Items should be returned on or before the date shown below. Items
not already requested by other borrowers may be renewed in person,
in writing or by telephone. To renew, please quote the number on the
barcode label. To renew online a PIN is required. This can be requested
at your local library.
Renew online @ **www.dublincitypubliclibraries.ie**
Fines charged for overdue items will include postage incurred in recovery.
Damage to or loss of items will be charged to the borrower.

Leabharlanna Poiblí Chathair Bhaile Átha Cliath
Dublin City Public Libraries

Comhairle Cathrach
Bhaile Átha Cliath
Dublin City Council

PEARSE STREET BRANCH
BRAINSE SRÁID PIARSACH
TEL: 6744888

Due Date	Due Date	Due Date
3 0 JAN 2019		

THE ⚜ TIMES
GREAT
QUOTATIONS

Published by Times Books
An imprint of HarperCollins Publishers
Westerhill Road
Bishopbriggs
Glasgow G64 2QT

www.harpercollins.co.uk
times.books@harpercollins.co.uk

First edition 2018

A catalogue record for this book is available from the British Library.

ISBN 978-0-00-831361-6

10 9 8 7 6 5 4 3 2 1

Printed and bound in Great Britain by CPI Group (UK) Ltd,
Croydon, CR0 4YY

Cover image © Bettmann / Getty

Our thanks and acknowledgements go to Lily Cox and Robin Ashton
at News Syndication and, in particular, at The Times, Ian Brunskill
and, at HarperCollins, Gerry Breslin, Jethro Lennox, Karen Midgley,
Kerry Ferguson, Sarah Woods and Evelyn Sword.

CONTENTS

INTRODUCTION

"A good newspaper," said the writer Arthur Miller, "is a nation talking to itself." Being a good newspaper, *The Times* strives to be exactly that ideal. Being intelligent, too, it realised some years ago that one way to promote that end was to make use of the words of interesting people talking to others. As a consequence, in the Daily Universal Register section of every edition, next to the birthdays, the anniversaries and the plashings of voles, there began to appear a stimulating quotation or saying of note, of which this volume is a selection.

Because the quotes which have appeared in the newspaper were assembled on random lines, this is not intended to be a traditional, comprehensive dictionary of famous quotations as such, though I hope it is nevertheless a valuable work of reference. Rather, the content has been grouped into common themes. Again, the hope is that, taken together in this way, these insights, musings and witty observations will provide food for thought. Those readers who wish to find quotes from specific people can easily do so by consulting the index at the back of the book.

Winston Churchill, the originator of a memorable line or two himself, believed it "a good thing for an uneducated man to read books of quotations". He may have been playing up his own inattentiveness as a schoolboy, but what can the rest of us gain from a ramble through the thoughts of greater minds?
One thing is that they do think alike. Over the centuries, the same subjects and reflections recur, for after all much is constant in the human race. Often, too, even the words are similar, and at certain times in history seem to occur to people almost simultaneously. Was it William Faulkner or André Gide

who said something about not being able to swim for new horizons without losing sight of the shore?

And, besides being treated to some world-class lectures in the essentials of philosophy, politics, success and common sense, there is the satisfaction (and surprise) of discovering how many expressions that we use every day are actually quotations. Who first said he was going from the sublime to the ridiculous? Napoleon, while leaving Russia. Who held that hell could be paved with good resolutions (often misquoted as good intentions)? That was Mark Twain. And was it a logistics company or the polar explorer Fridtjof Nansen who advised that the difficult takes a little time, the impossible a little longer?

Similarly, it is good to be reminded of the proper context of phrases often cited without knowledge of to what they refer. Making the pips squeak, a favourite standby of politicians, initially had nothing to do with taxing the rich. It was coined in 1918 with regard to the scale of German reparations for the First World War.

When Stanley Baldwin talked of newspapers having "power without responsibility", he was himself quoting his cousin Rudyard Kipling, and when his successor as prime minister returned from Germany holding in his hand "peace with honour", he was referencing a remark of his mid-19th century predecessor, Lord John Russell.

In the preparation of the text, every effort has been made to attribute correctly the quotations chosen. Their sources have been given where they are known to be contemporaneous with or authored by the speaker. Where it might be helpful, an English translation is given from a foreign language.

Remembrance of Things Past? Nothing to do with Proust originally, it comes from a Shakespeare sonnet. Fools rush in; hope springs eternal; to err is human; even that Cup Final favourite sing-song about death's sting – all 18th century poet Alexander Pope. Let us salute Samuel Johnson as a compiler of dictionaries, but I can't agree with him that making – and reading – them is "dull work".

James Owen

GREAT
QUOTATIONS

ACHIEVEMENT AND SUCCESS

He who does something at the head of one regiment,
will eclipse him who does nothing at the head of a hundred.
[Letter, 1861]
Abraham Lincoln, 16th president of the US (1809–1865)

·

Those who believe that they are exclusively in the right are
generally those who achieve something.
Proper Studies (1927)
Aldous Huxley, English writer and philosopher (1894–1963)

·

Concentrate all of your thoughts upon the work at hand.
The sun's rays do not burn until brought to a focus.
Alexander Graham Bell, Scottish-born scientist and inventor
(1847–1922)

·

Give me but one firm spot on which to stand and I will move
the Earth.
Archimedes, Greek mathematician and physicist (287–212 BC)

·

Talent hits a target no one else can hit. Genius hits a target
no one else can see.
The World as Will and Representation (1819)
Arthur Schopenhauer, German philosopher (1788–1860)

For myself, losing is not coming second. It's getting out of the water knowing you could have done better.
Ian Thorpe, Australian Olympic swimmer (1982–)

•

One secret of success in life is for a man to be ready for his opportunity when it comes.
Benjamin Disraeli, prime minister of the UK (1804–1881)

•

Well done is better than well said.
Benjamin Franklin, founding father of the US (1706–1790)

•

To gain that which is worth having, it may be necessary to lose everything else.
The Price of My Soul (1969)
Bernadette Devlin McAliskey, Irish civil rights leader (1947–)

•

It is easier to live through someone else than to become complete yourself.
The Feminine Mystique (1963)
Betty Friedan, American writer and activist (1921–2006)

•

Discipline is the bridge between goals and accomplishment.
Mother Teresa, Albanian nun and missionary (1910–1997)

It's the stuff of dreams ... Kids from Kilburn don't become
favourite for the Tour de France. You're supposed to become
a postman or a milkman or work in Ladbrokes.
Bradley Wiggins, British professional road racing cyclist (1980–)

•

The fact that some geniuses were laughed at does not imply
that all who are laughed at are geniuses. They laughed at
Columbus, they laughed at Fulton, they laughed at the
Wright brothers. But they also laughed at Bozo the Clown.
Broca's Brain (1979)
Carl Sagan, American astronomer and educator (1934–1996)

•

Diligence is the mother of good fortune, and idleness,
its opposite, never led to good intention's goal.
Don Quixote (1605)
Miguel de Cervantes, Spanish writer (1547–1616)

•

The world is divided into people who do things and people
who get the credit. Try, if you can, to belong to the first class.
There's far less competition.
Dwight Morrow, American diplomat (1873–1931)

•

The two kinds of people on earth I mean are the people who lift,
and the people who lean.
Ella Wheeler Wilcox, American writer and poet (1850–1919)

I attribute my success to this — I never gave or took any excuse.
Florence Nightingale, English social reformer and nurse
(1820–1910)

·

The reasonable man adapts himself to the world; the unreasonable
one persists in trying to adapt the world to himself. Therefore all
progress depends on the unreasonable man.
Man and Superman (1903)
George Bernard Shaw, Irish playwright (1856–1950)

·

Success is more dangerous than failure, the ripples break over
a wider coastline.
Graham Greene, English writer (1904–1991)

·

If everyone is moving forward together, then success takes care
of itself.
Henry Ford, American industrialist and businessman (1863–1947)

·

Not in the clamour of the crowded street, not in the shouts and
plaudits of the throng, but in ourselves, are triumph and defeat.
Henry Wadsworth Longfellow, American poet (1807–1882)

·

Fame is no plant that grows on mortal soil.
Lycidas (1637)
John Milton, English poet (1608–1674)

All the world's great have been little boys who wanted the moon.
Cup of Gold (1929)
John Steinbeck, American writer (1902–1968)

•

Whether our efforts are, or not, favoured by life, let us be able
to say when we come near the great goal, "I have done what
I could".
Louis Pasteur, French biologist and chemist (1822–1895)

•

I never see what has been done; I only see what remains
to be done.
Marie Curie, French-Polish physicist and chemist (1867–1934)

•

All you need in this life is ignorance and confidence;
then success is sure.
Mark Twain, American writer (1835–1910)

•

To live at all is miracle enough.
Mervyn Peake, English writer (1911–1968)

•

In most things success depends on knowing how long it takes
to succeed.
Pensées et fragments inédits
Montesquieu, French political philosopher (1689–1755)

The reward of a thing well done is to have done it.
New England Reformers (1844)
Ralph Waldo Emerson, American poet, essayist and philosopher
(1803–1882)

•

The love of life is necessary to the vigorous prosecution of any
undertaking.
Samuel Johnson, English writer, critic and lexicographer (1709–1784)

•

I had done all that I could; and no man is well pleased to have
his all neglected, be it ever so little.
Samuel Johnson, English writer, critic and lexicographer (1709–1784)

•

It is not the mountain we conquer, but ourselves.
Sir Edmund Hillary, New Zealand mountaineer (1919–2008)

•

We may become the makers of our fate when we have ceased to
pose as its prophets.
Sir Karl Popper, Austrian-British philosopher and professor
(1902–1994)

•

All men who have turned out worth anything have had the chief
hand in their own education.
[Letter to JG Lockhart, 1830]
Sir Walter Scott, Scottish writer (1771–1832)

My mountain did not seem to me a lifeless thing of rock and ice, but warm and friendly and living.
She was a mother hen, and the other mountains were chicks under her wings.
Man of Everest (1955)
Tenzing Norgay, Nepali Sherpa mountaineer (1914–1986)

•

Many of life's failures are people who did not realise how close they were to success when they gave up.
Thomas Edison, American inventor (1847–1931)

•

Genius is one per cent inspiration, ninety-nine per cent perspiration.
Thomas Edison, American inventor (1847–1931)

•

It is sobering to consider that when Mozart was my age he had already been dead for a year.
Tom Lehrer, American humourist and singer-songwriter (1928–)

•

Success is relative: It is what we can make of the mess we have made of things.
The Family Reunion (1939)
TS Eliot, English-American poet, critic and dramatist (1888–1965)

In the United States there's a Puritan ethic and a mythology of success. He who is successful is good. In Latin countries, in Catholic countries, a successful person is a sinner.
International Herald Tribune (1988)
Umberto Eco, Italian philosopher, writer and professor of semiotics (1932–2016)

•

Great things are not done by impulse, but by a series of small things brought together.
Vincent van Gogh, Dutch painter (1853–1890)

•

I felt as if I was walking with destiny, and that all my past life had been but a preparation for this hour and this trial.
[On becoming prime minister during the Second World War]
Sir Winston Churchill, prime minister of the UK, historian and Nobel Prize winner (1874–1965)

ACTING AND DRAMA

Just say the lines and don't trip over the furniture.
Sir Noël Coward, English playwright (1899–1973)

•

Television has brought back murder into the home —
where it belongs.
Alfred Hitchcock, English film director (1899–1980)

•

If in the first act you have hung a pistol on the wall, then
in the following one it should be fired. Otherwise don't put
it there.
Teatr i iskusstvo (1904)
Anton Chekhov, Russian playwright and short-story writer
(1860–1904)

•

The structure of a play is always the story of how the birds
came home to roost.
Shadows of the Gods (1958)
Arthur Miller, American playwright (1915–2005)

•

The basic essential of a great actor is that he loves himself
in acting.
My Autobiography (1964)
Charlie Chaplin, English comic actor, director and composer
(1889–1977)

Without wonder and insight, acting is just a trade.
With it, it becomes creation.
The Lonely Life (1962)
Bette Davis, American actress (1908–1989)

•

You spend all your life trying to do something they put people
in asylums for.
Jane Fonda, American actress (1937–)

•

Acting should be like punk in the best way. It should be a full-on
expression of self – only without the broken bottles.
Uncut (2000)
John Cusack, American actor (1966–)

•

Playing Shakespeare is very tiring. You never get to sit down,
unless you're a king.
Josephine Hull, American actress (1877–1957)

•

Acting is a masochistic form of exhibitionism. It is not quite
the occupation of an adult.
Time (1978)
Laurence Olivier, English actor (1907–1989)

A painter paints, a musician plays, a writer writes –
but a movie actor waits.
A Life on Film (1967)
Mary Astor, American actress (1906–1987)

•

Acting is standing up naked and turning around slowly.
Life Is a Banquet (1977)
Rosalind Russell, American actress (1907–1976)

•

Being another character is more interesting than being yourself.
Sir John Gielgud, English actor (1904–2000)

•

The art of acting consists in keeping people from coughing.
Sir Ralph Richardson, English actor (1902–1983)

ACTIONS AND BEHAVIOUR

Official dignity tends to increase in inverse ratio to the importance of the country in which the office is held.
Beyond the Mexique Bay (1934)
Aldous Huxley, English writer and philosopher (1894–1963)

•

Most human beings have an almost infinite capacity for taking things for granted.
Themes and Variations (1950)
Aldous Huxley, English writer and philosopher (1894–1963)

•

It is always easier to fight for one's principles than to live up to them.
Alfred Adler, Austrian psychologist and psychiatrist (1870–1937)

•

Man is so made that he can only find relaxation from one kind of labour by taking up another.
The Crime of Sylvestre Bonnard (1881)
Anatole France, French poet (1844–1924)

•

A man's mind will very generally refuse to make itself up until it be driven and compelled by emergency.
Ayala's Angel (1881)
Anthony Trollope, English writer (1815–1882)

I have taken great care not to laugh at human actions, not to weep at them, nor to hate them, but to understand them.
Tractatus Politicus (1677)
Baruch Spinoza, Dutch philosopher (1632–1677)

•

Men who are unhappy, like men who sleep badly, are always proud of the fact.
The Conquest of Happiness (1930)
Bertrand Russell, British philosopher, mathematician, historian, and writer (1872–1970)

•

One of the symptoms of approaching nervous breakdown is the belief that one's work is terribly important, and that to take a holiday would bring all kinds of disaster.
In Praise of Idleness and Other Essays (1935)
Bertrand Russell, British philosopher, mathematician, historian, and writer (1872–1970)

•

The pendulum of the mind oscillates between sense and nonsense, not between right and wrong.
Memories, Dreams, Reflections (1962)
Carl Jung, Swiss psychologist (1875–1961)

The shoe that fits one person pinches another; there is no recipe for living that suits all cases.
Modern Man in Search of a Soul (1933)
Carl Jung, Swiss psychologist (1875–1961)

•

Where we have strong emotions, we're liable to fool ourselves.
Cosmos (1980)
Carl Sagan, American astronomer and educator (1934–1996)

•

My life is spent in a perpetual alternation between two rhythms, the rhythm of attracting people for fear I may be lonely, and the rhythm of trying to get rid of them because I know that I am bored.
The Observer (1948)
CEM Joad, English philosopher (1891–1953)

•

Any man may be in good spirits and good temper when he's well dressed. There ain't much credit in that.
Martin Chuzzlewit (1844)
Charles Dickens, English writer and social critic (1812–1870)

•

Every one says forgiveness is a lovely idea, until they have something to forgive.
Mere Christianity (1952)
CS Lewis, British literary scholar and writer (1898–1963)

Pleasure is a thief to business.
The Complete English Tradesman (1726)
Daniel Defoe, English trader, writer and spy (1660–1731)

•

The heart of man is made to reconcile the most glaring
contradictions.
Essays and Treatises on Several Subjects (1753)
David Hume, Scottish philosopher (1711–1776)

•

Every time you open your wardrobe, you look at your clothes
and you wonder what you are going to wear. What you are really
saying is, "Who am I going to be today?"
The New Yorker (1995)
Fay Weldon, English feminist and playwright (1931–)

•

Everyone thinks his own burden is heavy.
French proverb

•

The smyler with the knyf under the cloke.
The Knight's Tale (1387)
Geoffrey Chaucer, English poet (c. 1343–1400)

•

Our deeds determine us, as much as we determine our deeds.
Adam Bede (1859)
George Eliot, English writer (1819–1880)

Our actions are like ships which we may watch set out to sea, and not know when or with what cargo they will return to port.
The Bell (1958)
Iris Murdoch, Irish writer (1919–1999)

•

The world can only be grasped by action, not by contemplation ...
The hand is the cutting edge of the mind.
The Ascent of Man (1973)
Jacob Bronowski, British-Polish mathematician and science historian (1908–1974)

•

Only the actions of the just,
Smell sweet and blossom on their dust.
The Contention of Ajax and Ulysses for the Armour of Achilles (1659)
James Shirley, English playwright (1596–1666)

•

It isn't what we say or think that defines us, but what we do.
Sense and Sensibility (1811)
Jane Austen, English writer (1775–1817)

•

I was raised to feel that doing nothing was a sin. I had to learn to do nothing.
The Observer (1998)
Jenny Joseph, English poet (1932–2018)

It is impossible to enjoy idling thoroughly unless one has plenty of work to do.
Idle Thoughts of an Idle Fellow (1886)
Jerome K Jerome, English writer (1859–1927)

•

Deeds, not words shall speak me.
The Lover's Progress (1647)
John Fletcher, English playwright (1579–1625)

•

I have always thought the actions of men the best interpreters of their thoughts.
An Essay Concerning Human Understanding (1689)
John Locke, English philosopher (1632–1704)

•

Word is but wynd; leff woord and tak the dede.
Secrets of Old Philosophers
John Lydgate, English poet (1370–1451)

•

The highest reward for a man's toil is not what he gets for it but what he becomes by it.
John Ruskin, English art critic (1819–1900)

Action is consolatory. It is the enemy of thought and the friend of flattering illusions.
Nostromo (1904)
Joseph Conrad, Polish-British writer (1857–1924)

•

Iron rusts from disuse, stagnant water loses its purity, and in cold weather becomes frozen; even so does inaction sap the vigour of the mind.
The Notebooks of Leonardo da Vinci (1883)
Leonardo da Vinci, Italian polymath (1452–1519)

•

Everybody, sooner or later, sits down to a banquet of consequences.
Old Mortality (1884)
Robert Louis Stevenson, Scottish writer (1850–1894)

•

The only infallible rule we know is, that the man who is always talking about being a gentleman never is one.
Ask Mamma (1858)
RS Surtees, English editor and sporting writer (1805–1864)

•

Everyone is more or less mad on one point.
Plain Tales from the Hills (1888)
Rudyard Kipling, English journalist and writer (1865–1936)

The ordinary acts we practise every day at home are of more importance to the soul than their simplicity might suggest.
Sir Thomas More, English saint and lawyer (1478–1535)

•

Terror ... often arises from a pervasive sense of disestablishment; that things are in the unmaking.
Danse Macabre (1981)
Stephen King, American writer (1947–)

•

Perfection is terrible, it cannot have children.
The Munich Mannequins (1965)
Sylvia Plath, American poet and writer (1932–1963)

•

It is part of human nature to hate the man you have hurt.
Agricola (c. 98)
Tacitus, Roman senator and historian (c. 56–120)

•

Considering how foolishly people act and how pleasantly they prattle, perhaps it would be better for the world if they talked more and did less.
A Writer's Notebook (1946)
W Somerset Maugham, British playwright (1874–1965)

It is an undoubted truth, that the less one has to do, the less time one finds to do it in. One yawns, one procrastinates, one can do it when one will, and therefore one seldom does it at all.
Lord Chesterfield, British statesman (1694–1773)

·

Anything that is worth doing has been done frequently.
Things hitherto undone should be given, I suspect, a wide berth.
Mainly on the Air (1946)
Sir Max Beerbohm, English essayist and parodist (1872–1956)

·

Truly, when the day of judgment comes, it will not be a question of what we have read, but what we have done.
De Imitatione Christi (c. 1418–1427)
Thomas á Kempis, Dutch-German canon regular and writer (1380–1471)

·

Men are rewarded and punished not for what they do, but rather for how their acts are defined. This is why men are more interested in better justifying themselves than in better behaving themselves.
The Second Sin (1973)
Thomas Szasz, American-Hungarian psychiatrist (1920–2012)

ADVICE AND PRINCIPLES

Out of clutter, find simplicity.
Albert Einstein, German theoretical physicist (1879–1955)

•

There's only one corner of the universe you can be certain of
improving, and that's your own self.
Time Must Have a Stop (1944)
Aldous Huxley, English writer and philosopher (1894–1963)

•

Start where you are. Use what you have. Do what you can.
Arthur Ashe, American tennis player and Aids activist (1943–1993)

•

If you would be known, and not know, vegetate in a village;
if you would know, and not be known, live in a city.
Lacon (1820)
Charles Caleb Colton, English cleric (1780–1832)

•

Reflect upon your present blessings, of which every man has
many; not on your past misfortunes of which all men have some.
Charles Dickens, English writer and social critic (1812–1870)

•

Never make a defence or apology before you be accused.
Charles I, King of England (1600–1649)

When environment changes, there must be a corresponding change in life.
The Wartime Journals (1970)
Charles Lindbergh, American aviator (1902–1974)

•

Get the advice of everybody whose advice is worth having —
they are very few — and then do what you think best yourself.
Charles Stewart Parnell, Irish nationalist leader (1846–1891)

•

A ruffled mind makes a restless pillow.
Charlotte Brontë, English writer (1816–1855)

•

If you have a garden and a library, you have everything you need.
Ad Familiares IX, 4
Cicero, Roman statesman (106–43 BC)

•

Stand a little less between me and the sun.
[On being asked by Alexander the Great what he could do for him]
Diogenes, Greek philosopher (412–323 BC)

•

Hope is a good breakfast but a bad supper.
Francis Bacon, English philosopher, statesman and essayist
(1561–1626)

Be wisely worldly, but not worldly wise.
Francis Quarles, English poet (1592–1644)

•

Believe me! The secret of reaping the greatest fruitfulness and the greatest enjoyment from life is to live dangerously!
Die fröhliche Wissenschaft (1882)
Friedrich Nietzsche, German philosopher and writer (1844–1900)

•

Simplicity is light, carefree, neat and loving — not a self-punishing ascetic trip.
A Place in Space (1995)
Gary Snyder, American poet (1930–)

•

Take care to get what you like or you will be forced to like what you get.
Man and Superman (1903)
George Bernard Shaw, Irish playwright (1856–1950)

•

We must consult our means rather than our wishes.
George Washington, 1st president of the US (1732–1799)

•

One sees great things from the valley; only small things from the peak.
GK Chesterton, English writer (1874–1936)

Be steady and well-ordered in your life so that you can be fierce
and original in your work.
Gustave Flaubert, French writer (1821–1880)

•

This is the precept by which I have lived: prepare for the worst;
expect the best; and take what comes.
Hannah Arendt, American-German philosopher (1906–1975)

•

Up with your damned nonsense will I put twice, or perhaps once,
but sometimes always, by God, never.
Hans Richter, Hungarian-born conductor and painter (1888–1976)

•

Live all you can: it's a mistake not to. It doesn't matter what you
do in particular, so long as you have had your life. If you haven't
had that, what have you had?
Henry James, American writer (1843–1916)

•

Never trust the man who tells you all his troubles but keeps from
you all his joys.
Jewish proverb

•

Meetings are a great trap ... However, they are indispensable
when you don't want to do anything.
Ambassador's Journal (1969)
JK Galbraith, Canadian economist (1908–2006)

Things which matter most must never be at the mercy of things which matter least.
Johann Wolfgang von Goethe, German writer and statesman (1749–1832)

•

Praising all alike is praising none.
A Letter To A Lady
John Gay, English poet (1685–1732)

•

Nor love thy life, nor hate; but what thou liv'st live well, how long or short permit to heaven.
Paradise Lost (1667)
John Milton, English poet (1608–1674)

•

Though I am always in haste, I am never in a hurry.
John Wesley, English cleric (1703–1791)

•

Blessed is he who expects nothing, for he shall never be disappointed.
Jonathan Swift, Irish poet and satirist (1667–1745)

•

A thick skin is a gift from God.
Konrad Adenauer, chancellor of Germany (1876–1967)

Civility costs nothing and buys everything.
Lady Mary Wortley Montagu, English writer (1689–1762)

•

The strongest of all warriors are these two — Time and Patience.
Leo Tolstoy, Russian writer (1828–1910)

•

If you don't know where you are going, any road will get
you there.
Lewis Carroll, English writer (1832–1898)

•

A proverb is one man's wit and all men's wisdom.
Lord John Russell, prime minister of the UK (1792–1878)

•

Turn your face to the sun and the shadows fall behind you.
Maori proverb

•

The heart that gives, gathers.
Marianne Moore, American poet (1887–1972)

•

You will find it a very good practice always to verify your
references, sir!
Martin Joseph Routh, English classical scholar (1755–1854)

The sense of being well-dressed gives a feeling of inward tranquillity which religion is powerless to bestow.
Emerson, Social Aims (1876)
Miss CF Forbes, English writer (1817–1911)

•

Be yourself; everyone else is already taken.
Oscar Wilde, Irish dramatist and poet (1854–1900)

•

I always pass on good advice. It is the only thing to do with it. It is never of any use to oneself.
An Ideal Husband (1895)
Oscar Wilde, Irish dramatist and poet (1854–1900)

•

Education is what you get when you read the fine print; experience is what you get when you don't.
Pete Seeger, American folk singer (1919–2014)

•

When the bee comes to your house, let her have beer; you may want to visit the bee's house some day.
Proverb from the Republic of Congo

•

There was no need to do any housework at all. After the first four years the dirt doesn't get any worse.
The Naked Civil Servant (1968)
Quentin Crisp, English writer, raconteur and actor (1908–1999)

There is no such uncertainty as a sure thing.
Robert Burns, Scottish poet (1759–1796)

·

If you live among wolves you have to howl like a wolf.
Russian proverb

·

He who is blind, dumb and deaf will live a peaceful life
of a hundred years.
Sicilian proverb

·

You've got to have two out of death, sex and jewels.
[In *The Sunday Times*, 1994, on his principles for a successful
museum show]
Sir Roy Strong, English art historian (1935–)

·

Nature has given us two ears, two eyes, and but one tongue —
to the end that we should hear and see more than we speak.
Socrates, Greek philosopher (470–399 BC)

·

There are two possible situations — one can either do this
or that. My honest opinion and my friendly advice is this:
do it or do not do it — you will regret both.
Either/Or (1843)
Søren Kierkegaard, Danish philosopher (1813–1855)

Don't speak unless you can improve on the silence.
Spanish proverb

•

The shrimp that falls asleep is carried away by the current.
Spanish proverb

•

Straightforwardness without civility is like a surgeon's knife,
effective but unpleasant. Candour with courtesy is helpful and
admirable.
Sri Yukteswar Giri, Indian guru (1855–1936)

•

Shared joy is a double joy; shared sorrow is half a sorrow.
Swedish proverb

•

Coffee should be black as hell, strong as death and sweet as love.
Turkish proverb

•

Your head is not only for putting a hat on.
Ukrainian proverb

•

Think like a wise man but express yourself like the
common people.
WB Yeats, Irish poet (1865–1939)

Be nice to people on your way up because you'll meet
'em on your way down.
Wilson Mizner, American playwright (1876–1933)

•

Let our advance worrying become advance thinking and
planning.
Sir Winston Churchill, prime minister of the UK, historian and
Nobel Prize winner (1874–1965)

APPETITES

Time for a little something.
Winnie the Pooh (1926)
AA Milne, English writer (1882–1956)

•

In the spring a livelier iris changes on the burnished dove;
In the spring a young man's fancy lightly turns to thoughts
of love.
Locksley Hall (1842)
Alfred, Lord Tennyson, English poet (1809–1892)

•

My problem lies in reconciling my gross habits with
my net income.
Errol Flynn, Australian-born actor (1909–1959)

•

There is no love sincerer than the love of food.
Man and Superman (1903)
George Bernard Shaw, Irish playwright (1856–1950)

•

People say I wasted my money. I say 90 per cent went
on women, fast cars and booze. The rest I wasted.
George Best, Northern Irish professional footballer
(1946–2005)

Three glasses of wine drive away the evil spirits, but with the fourth they return.
German proverb

·

If all be true that I do think,
There are five reasons we should drink:
Good wine — a friend — or being dry —
Or lest we should be by and by —
Or any other reason why.
Five Reasons for Drinking (1689)
Henry Aldrich, English philosopher and composer (1647–1710)

·

We drink one another's healths, and spoil our own.
Idle Thoughts of an Idle Fellow (1886)
Jerome K Jerome, English writer (1859–1927)

·

No pleasure is worth giving up for the sake of two more years in a geriatric home in Weston-super-Mare.
The Times (1994)
[Attr.]
Kingsley Amis, English writer and critic (1922–1995)

·

Wine may well be considered the most healthful and most hygienic of beverages.
Études sur le vin (1866)
Louis Pasteur, French biologist and chemist (1822–1895)

One reason why I don't drink is because I wish to know when I am having a good time.
Christian Herald (1960)
Nancy Astor, American-born politician and socialite (1879–1964)

•

Strange to see how a good dinner and feasting reconciles everybody.
Diary (1660)
Samuel Pepys, English diarist, naval administrator and politician (1633–1703)

•

Hath wine an oblivious power? Can it pluck out the sting from the brain? The draught might beguile for an hour, But still leaves behind it the pain.
Anonymous

•

A well-balanced person has a drink in each hand.
Gullible's Travels (1982)
Sir Billy Connolly, Scottish comedian (1942–)

•

Too much and too little wine. Give him none, he cannot find truth; give him too much, the same.
Pensées (1670)
Blaise Pascal, French mathematician and physicist (1623–1662)

There are two things that will be believed of any man
whatsoever, and one of them is that he has taken to drink.
Penrod (1914)
Booth Tarkington, American writer and dramatist (1869–1946)

•

I only take a drink on two occasions – when I'm thirsty
and when I'm not.
Brendan Behan, Irish writer (1923–1964)

•

Every form of addiction is bad, no matter whether the narcotic
be alcohol or morphine or idealism.
Memories, Dreams, Reflections (1962)
Carl Jung, Swiss psychologist (1875–1961)

•

Then trust me, there's nothing like drinking
So pleasant on this side the grave;
It keeps the unhappy from thinking,
And makes e'en the valiant more brave.
Nothing like Grog (1841)
Charles Dibdin, British composer (1745–1814)

•

Bring in the bottled lightning, a clean tumbler,
and a corkscrew.
Nicholas Nickleby (1838)
Charles Dickens, English writer and social critic
(1812–1870)

We are fighting Germany, Austria and drink, and so far
as I can see the greatest of these deadly foes is drink.
[Speech at Bangor, 1915]
David Lloyd George, prime minister of the UK (1863–1945)

•

I feel sorry for people who don't drink. When they wake up in
the morning, that's the best they are going to feel all day.
Dean Martin, American singer and actor (1917–1995)

•

One whisky is all right; two is too much; three is too few.
A Taste of Scotch (1989)
Derek Cooper, British journalist and broadcaster (1925–2014)

•

Come quickly, I am tasting stars!
[On discovering he had created champagne]
Dom Perignon, French Benedictine monk (1638–1715)

•

An alcoholic is someone you don't like who drinks as much
as you do.
Dylan Thomas, Welsh writer (1914–1953)

•

To eat figs off the tree in the very early morning, when they have
been barely touched by the sun, is one of the exquisite pleasures
of the Mediterranean.
Italian Food (1954)
Elizabeth David, British cookery writer (1913–1992)

Great eaters of meat are in general more cruel and ferocious than other men. The English are known for their cruelty.
Émile (1762)
Jean-Jacques Rousseau, Genevan philosopher (1712–1778)

•

Food is an important part of a balanced diet.
Metropolitan Life (1978)
Fran Lebowitz, American writer and public speaker (1950–)

•

A cheerful look makes a dish a feast.
Jacula Prudentum (1640)
George Herbert, Welsh-born poet and priest (1593–1633)

•

Man cannot live by bread alone; he must have peanut butter.
[Inaugural address, 1881]
James A Garfield, 20th president of the US (1831–1881)

•

I saw him even now going the way of all flesh, that is to say towards the kitchen.
Westward Hoe (1607)
John Webster, English dramatist (c. 1580–1634)

•

Coffee is a cold dry food, suited to the ascetic life and sedative of lust.
Katib Chelebi, Ottoman scholar (1609–1657)

All my life I have been a very thirsty person.
The Sunday Times (2001)
Keith Floyd, British cook, restaurateur and television personality (1943–2009)

•

The noblest of all dogs is the hot-dog; it feeds the hand that bites it.
Quotations for Our Time (1977)
Laurence J Peter, Canadian educator (1919–1990)

•

Good mashed potato is one of the great luxuries of life and I don't blame Elvis for eating it every night for the last year of his life.
In Praise of the Potato (1989)
Lindsey Bareham, British cookery writer

ASPIRATION AND OPPORTUNITY

Now, gentlemen, let us do something today which the world may talk of hereafter.
Admiral Cuthbert Collingwood, admiral of the Royal Navy (1748–1810)

•

We have to do the best we can. This is our sacred human responsibility.
Albert Einstein, German theoretical physicist (1879–1955)

•

Come, my friends. 'Tis not too late to seek a newer world.
Ulysses (1833)
Alfred, Lord Tennyson, English poet (1809–1892)

•

One does not discover new lands without consenting to lose sight, for a very long time, of the shore.
Les faux-monnayeurs (1925)
André Gide, French writer (1869–1951)

•

A goal without a plan is just a wish.
Antoine de Saint-Exupéry, French writer (1900–1944)

Nurture your minds with great thoughts; to believe in the heroic makes heroes.
Benjamin Disraeli, prime minister of the UK (1804–1881)

•

We are not creatures of circumstance; we are creators of circumstance.
Benjamin Disraeli, prime minister of the UK (1804–1881)

•

There comes a time in a man's life when to get where he has to go — if there are no doors or windows — he walks through a wall.
Rembrandt's Hat (1972)
Bernard Malamud, American writer (1914–1986)

•

By prevailing over all obstacles and distractions, one may unfailingly arrive at his chosen goal or destination.
Christopher Columbus, Italian explorer (1451–1506)

•

In order to carry a positive action we must develop here a positive vision.
Dalai Lama, Tibetan monk of the Gelug school (1935–)

•

Small opportunities are often the beginning of great enterprises.
Against Leptines (c. 385/4 BC)
Demosthenes, Greek orator and Athenian statesman (c. 384–322 BC)

Nobody made a greater mistake than he who did nothing because he could do only a little.
Edmund Burke, Irish philosopher and statesman (1729–1797)

•

I am only one, but I am one. I cannot do everything, but I can do something. And I will not let what I cannot do interfere with what I can do.
Edward Everett Hale, American writer (1822–1909)

•

What we're saying today is that you're either part of the solution or you're part of the problem.
[Speech in San Francisco, 1968]
Eldridge Cleaver, American political activist (1935–1998)

•

I am here to live out loud.
Émile Zola, French writer (1840–1902)

•

Man's main task in life is to give birth to himself, to become what he potentially is. The most important product of his effort is his own personality.
Man for Himself (1947)
Erich Fromm, German philosopher and psychologist (1900–1980)

You see things; and you say, "Why?" But I dream things that never were; and I say, "Why not?"
Methuselah (1903)
George Bernard Shaw, Irish playwright (1856–1950)

•

It will never rain roses: when we want to have more roses, we must plant more roses.
George Eliot, English writer (1819–1880)

•

What do we live for, if it is not to make life less difficult for each other?
Middlemarch (1871–72)
George Eliot, English writer (1819–1880)

•

Life is either a daring adventure or nothing.
Let Us Have Faith (1940)
Helen Keller, American writer and social reformer (1880–1968)

•

It is better to fail in originality than to succeed in imitation.
Herman Melville, American writer (1819–1891)

•

Time is that wherein there is opportunity, and opportunity is that wherein there is no great time.
Hippocrates, Greek physician (460–370 BC)

He who has begun has half done. Dare to be wise; begin.
Epistles (20 BC)
Horace, Roman poet (65–8 BC)

•

You have not lived today until you have done something for
someone who can never repay you.
John Bunyan, English writer (1628–1688)

•

All this will not be finished in the first 100 days. Nor will
it be finished in the first 1,000 days, nor in the life of this
administration, nor even perhaps in our lifetime on this planet.
But let us begin.
[Inaugural address, 1961]
John F Kennedy, 35th president of the US (1917–1963)

•

What happens to a dream deferred?
Does it dry up
Like a raisin in the sun?
Langston Hughes, American poet (1902–1967)

•

The journey of a thousand miles begins with a single step.
Tao Te Ching
Lao Tzu, Chinese philosopher (?–533 BC)

Great fires erupt from tiny sparks.
Libyan proverb

•

Never doubt that a small group of thoughtful, committed citizens
can change the world. In fact, it's the only thing that ever has.
Margaret Mead, American anthropologist (1901–1978)

•

We must believe that we are gifted for something, and that this
thing, at whatever cost, must be attained.
Marie Curie, French-Polish physicist and chemist (1867–1934)

•

What can stop the determined heart and resolved will of man?
Frankenstein (1823)
Mary Shelley, English writer (1797–1851)

•

Life loves to be taken by the lapel and told: I'm with you kid.
Let's go.
Maya Angelou, American writer (1928–2014)

•

Chance is always powerful. Let your hook be always cast.
In the pool where you least expect it, will be fish.
Ovid, Roman poet (43 BC–AD 18)

I am always doing that which I cannot do, in order that I may learn how to do it.
Pablo Picasso, Spanish painter (1881–1973)

•

Always do what you are afraid to do.
Ralph Waldo Emerson, American poet, essayist and philosopher (1803–1882)

•

Nothing great was ever achieved without enthusiasm.
Circles (1841)
Ralph Waldo Emerson, American poet, essayist and philosopher (1803–1882)

•

Here is a test to find whether your mission on earth is finished: if you're alive, it isn't.
Illusions: The Adventures of a Reluctant Messiah (1977)
Richard Bach, American writer (1936–)

•

The scouts' motto is founded on my initials, it is Be Prepared, which means, you are always to be in a state of readiness in mind and body to do your duty.
Scouting for Boys (1908)
Robert Baden-Powell, British Army officer (1857–1941)

Ah, but a man's reach should exceed his grasp,
Or what's a heaven for?
Andrea del Sarto (1855)
Robert Browning, English poet (1812–1889)

•

To be what we are, and to become what we are capable
of becoming, is the only end of life.
Robert Louis Stevenson, Scottish writer (1850–1894)

•

At the age of six I wanted to be a cook. At seven I wanted
to be Napoleon. And my ambition has been growing steadily
ever since.
Salvador Dalí, Spanish surrealist painter (1904–1989)

•

Nothing will ever be attempted if all possible objections must
first be overcome.
Samuel Johnson, English writer, critic and lexicographer (1709–1784)

•

If you are not criticised, you may not be doing much.
Human Life (1819)
Samuel Rogers, English poet (1763–1855)

•

To show your true ability is always, in a sense, to surpass
the limits of your ability, to go a little beyond them.
Simone de Beauvoir, French writer (1908–1986)

One sometimes finds what one is not looking for.
Sir Alexander Fleming, Scottish physician (1881–1955)

•

Strive for perfection in everything you do. Take the best
that exists and make it better. When it does not exist,
design it.
Sir Henry Royce, English engineer (1863–1933)

•

Either I will find a way, or I will make one.
Sir Philip Sidney, English poet (1554–1586)

•

Opportunities multiply as they are seized.
Sun Tzu, Chinese strategist (545–470 BC)

•

Believe you can and you're halfway there.
Theodore Roosevelt, 26th president of the US (1858–1919)

•

I wish to preach, not the doctrine of ignoble ease, but the
doctrine of the strenuous life.
[Speech in Chicago, 1899]
Theodore Roosevelt, 26th president of the US
(1858–1919)

Far better it is to dare mighty things, to win glorious triumphs, even though checkered by failure, than to rank with those poor spirits who neither enjoy much nor suffer much, because they live in that grey twilight that knows neither victory nor defeat.
[*The Strenuous Life* speech, 1899]
Theodore Roosevelt, 26th president of the US (1858–1919)

•

As you enter positions of trust and power, dream a little before you think.
[Commencement speech at Sarah Lawrence College, 1988]
Toni Morrison, American writer (1931–)

•

What would life be if we had no courage to attempt anything?
[Letter to his brother Theo, 1881]
Vincent van Gogh, Dutch painter (1853–1890)

•

The man who removes a mountain begins by carrying away small stones.
[Interview with *The Paris Review*, 1956]
William Faulkner, American writer (1897–1962)

•

You cannot swim for new horizons until you have courage to lose sight of the shore.
The Mansion (1959)
William Faulkner, American writer (1897–1962)

Things won are done; joy's soul lies in the doing.
Troilus and Cressida (1602)
William Shakespeare, English poet and dramatist
(1564–1616)

•

I would rather fail in a cause that will ultimately triumph
than to triumph in a cause that will ultimately fail.
[Campaign speech at New York State Fair Grounds,
Syracuse, 1912]
Woodrow Wilson, 28th president of the US (1856–1924)

•

A pessimist sees the difficulty in every opportunity;
an optimist sees the opportunity in every difficulty.
[Attr.]
Sir Winston Churchill, prime minister of the UK, historian and
Nobel Prize winner (1874–1965)

BELIEFS AND DOUBT

It is often said that there is no such thing as a free lunch.
The universe, however, is a free lunch.
Harper's Magazine (1994)
Alan Guth, American theoretical physicist (1947–)

•

Zen ... does not confuse spirituality with thinking about God
while one is peeling potatoes. Zen spirituality is just to peel
the potatoes.
The Way of Zen (1957)
Alan Watts, British teacher and writer (1915–1973)

•

My country, right or wrong; if right, to be kept right;
and if wrong, to be set right!
[Speech to the US Senate, 1872)
Carl Schurz, German revolutionary and American statesman
(1829–1906)

•

Men will wrangle for religion; write for it; fight for it; die for it;
anything but live for it.
Lacon (1820)
Charles Caleb Colton, English cleric (1780–1832)

Isn't it enough to see that a garden is beautiful without having to believe that there are fairies at the bottom of it too?
The Hitchhiker's Guide to the Galaxy (1979)
Douglas Adams, English humourist and dramatist (1952–2001)

•

Not things, but opinions about things, trouble men.
The Enchiridion of Epictetus (c. 125)
Epictetus, Greek philosopher (50–135)

•

At eighteen our convictions are hills from which we look;
at forty-five they are caves in which we hide.
Bernice Bobs her Hair (1920)
F Scott Fitzgerald, American writer (1896–1940)

•

All good moral philosophy is but a handmaid to religion.
The Advancement of Learning (1605)
Francis Bacon, English philosopher, statesman and essayist (1561–1626)

•

So long as man remains free he strives for nothing so incessantly and so painfully as to find someone to worship.
The Brothers Karamazov (1880)
Fyodor Dostoyevsky, Russian writer (1821–1881)

If the Devil doesn't exist, but man has created him, he has created him in his own likeness.
The Brothers Karamazov (1880)
Fyodor Dostoyevsky, Russian writer (1821–1881)

•

There is only one religion, though there are a hundred versions of it.
Plays Pleasant and Unpleasant (1898)
George Bernard Shaw, Irish playwright (1856–1950)

•

Religions are kept alive by heresies, which are really sudden explosions of faith. Dead religions do not produce them.
Thoughts in a Dry Season (1978)
Gerald Brenan, British writer (1894–1987)

•

If God is your emotional role model, very few human relationships will match up to it.
Oranges are Not the Only Fruit (1985)
Jeanette Winterson, English writer (1959–)

•

Religion, which should most distinguish us from the beasts, and ought most particularly elevate us, as rational creatures, above brutes, is that wherein men often appear most irrational, and more senseless than beasts.
An Essay Concerning Human Understanding (1689)
John Locke, English philosopher (1632–1704)

God and the doctor we alike adore
But only when in danger, not before;
The danger o'er, both are alike requited,
God is forgotten and the doctor slighted.
Epigrams (1677)
John Owen, Welsh epigrammist (1564–1622)

•

Human beings are perhaps never more frightening than when
they are convinced beyond doubt that they are right.
The Lost World of the Kalahari (1958)
Laurens van der Post, South African writer and political adviser
(1906–1996)

•

I see it as an elderly lady, who mutters away to herself in
a corner, ignored most of the time.
[In *Reader's Digest*, 1991, about the Church of England]
Lord Carey of Clifton, Archbishop of Canterbury (1935–)

•

To give light to them that sit in darkness and in the shadow
of death, to guide our feet into the way of peace.
The Bible
Luke 1:79

•

Man is quite insane. He wouldn't know how to create a maggot,
and he creates gods by the dozens.
Essais (1580)
Michel de Montaigne, French philosopher (1533–1592)

He who gains an indulgence is not, strictly speaking, absolved from the debt of punishment, but is given the means whereby he may pay it.
Summa Theologica (1485)
Saint Thomas Aquinas, Italian Catholic priest (1225–1274)

•

If the sun and moon should doubt, they'd immediately go out.
Auguries of Innocence (1863)
William Blake, English poet (1757–1827)

•

Both read the Bible day and night,
But thou read'st black where I read white.
The Everlasting Gospel (c. 1818)
William Blake, English poet (1757–1827)

•

It is a mistake to suppose that God is only, or even chiefly, concerned with religion.
William Temple, British theologian and Archbishop of Canterbury (1881–1944)

•

I am ready to meet my Maker. Whether my Maker is prepared for the great ordeal of meeting me is another matter.
Sir Winston Churchill, prime minister of the UK, historian and Nobel Prize winner (1874–1965)

Even God is deprived of this one thing only: the power to undo what has been done.
Agathon, Greek poet (448–400 BC)

•

God does not play dice.
The Born-Einstein Letters (1926)
Albert Einstein, German theoretical physicist (1879–1955)

•

I think it pisses God off if you walk by the color purple in a field somewhere and don't notice it.
The Color Purple (1985)
Alice Walker, American writer and activist (1944–)

•

In the beginning God created the heaven and the earth. And the earth was without form, and void; and darkness was upon the face of the deep. And the Spirit of God moved upon the face of the waters. And God said, Let there be light: and there was light.
The Bible
Genesis 1:2

•

God seems to have left the receiver off the hook, and time is running out.
The Ghost in the Machine (1967)
Arthur Koestler, Hungarian-British writer (1905–1983)

My dear child, you must believe in God in spite of what the clergy tell you.
Benjamin Jowett, English educator and theologian (1817–1893)

•

I cannot forgive Descartes; in all his philosophy he did his best to dispense with God. But he could not avoid making Him set the world in motion with a flick of His finger; after that he had no more use for God.
Pensées (1670)
Blaise Pascal, French mathematician and physicist (1623–1662)

•

In all important questions, man has learned to cope without recourse to God as a working hypothesis.
[Letter to a friend, 1944]
Dietrich Bonhoeffer, German pastor and theologian (1906–1945)

•

By Night an Atheist half believes a God.
Night-Thoughts on Life, Death and Immortality (1742–1745)
Edward Young, English poet (1683–1765)

•

God answers sharp and sudden on some prayers, And thrusts the thing we have prayed for in our face, A gauntlet with a gift in't.
Aurora Leigh (1857)
Elizabeth Barrett Browning, English poet (1806–1861)

So many gods, so many creeds,
So many paths that wind and wind,
While just the art of being kind
Is all the sad world needs.
The World's Need (1917)
Ella Wheeler Wilcox, American writer and poet (1850–1919)

•

God is a circle whose centre is everywhere and whose
circumference is nowhere.
Empedocles, Greek philosopher (495–444 BC)

CHALLENGE AND TENACITY

Man needs difficulties; they are necessary for health.
The Transcendent Function (1916)
Carl Jung, Swiss psychologist (1875–1961)

•

No easy problems ever come to the president of the
United States. If they are easy to solve, somebody else
has solved them.
Parade Magazine (1962)
Dwight D Eisenhower, 34th president of the US
(1890–1969)

•

Never stop because you are afraid — you are never so likely to be
wrong. Never keep a line of retreat; it is a wretched invention.
The difficult is what takes a little time; the impossible is what
takes a little longer.
Fridtjof Nansen, Norwegian polar explorer (1861–1930)

•

Security is when everything is settled, when nothing can
happen to you; security is the denial of life.
The Female Eunuch (1970)
Germaine Greer, Australian writer and intellectual (1939–)

Oft in danger, oft in woe,
Onward, Christians, onward go;
Bear the toil, maintain the strife,
Strengthened with the Bread of Life.
Oft in danger, oft in woe (1812)
H Kirke White, English poet (1785–1806)

.

Never give up, for that is just the place and time that the tide
will turn.
Old Town Folks (1869)
Harriet Beecher Stowe, American abolitionist and writer (1811–1896)

.

The drop of rain maketh a hole in the stone, not by violence
but by oft falling.
[Seventh Sermon before Edward VI, 1549]
Hugh Latimer, English Protestant martyr (1487–1555)

.

It is a common experience that a problem difficult at night
is resolved in the morning after the committee of sleep has
worked on it.
John Steinbeck, American writer (1902–1968)

.

Facing it, always facing it, that's the way to get through. Face it.
Typhoon (1902)
Joseph Conrad, Polish-British writer (1857–1924)

Nothing happens to anybody which he is not fitted by nature to bear.
Meditations (before 850)
Marcus Aurelius, Roman emperor (161–180)

•

Whoever said anybody has a right to give up?
Marian Wright Edelman, American children's rights activist (1939–)

•

I have been through some terrible things in my life, some of which actually happened.
Mark Twain, American writer (1835–1910)

•

You may not control all the events that happen to you but you can decide not to be reduced by them.
Letter to My Daughter (2008)
Maya Angelou, American writer (1928–2014)

•

There is no effort without error or shortcoming.
["Citizenship in a Republic" speech, 1910]
Theodore Roosevelt, 26th president of the US (1858–1919)

•

Fire is the test of gold; adversity, of strong men.
Moral Epistles (c. 65)
Seneca the Younger, Roman philosopher and poet (4 BC–AD 65)

Kites rise highest against the wind, not with it.
Sir Winston Churchill, prime minister of the UK, historian and
Nobel Prize winner (1874–1965)

•

If you bear the cross gladly, it will bear you.
De Imitatione Christi (c. 1418–1427)
Thomas á Kempis, Dutch-German canon regular and writer
(1380–1471)

•

When you have exhausted all possibilities, remember this —
you haven't.
Thomas Edison, American inventor (1847–1931)

CHANCE

Some people are so fond of ill luck that they run halfway
to meet it.
Douglas Jerrold, English playwright and journalist (1803–1857)

•

Luck is preparation meeting opportunity.
Oprah Winfrey, American talk show host and philanthropist
(1954–)

•

The more I practise the luckier I get.
Arnold Palmer, American professional golfer (1929–2016)

•

Luck is not chance, it's toil; fortune's expensive smile is earned.
Luck is not chance (1875)
Emily Dickinson, American poet (1830–1886)

•

Chance is always powerful. Let your hook be always cast.
In the pool where you least expect it, will be fish.
Heroides (c. 25–16 BC)
Ovid, Roman poet (43 BC–AD 18)

CHANGE

Change is not made without inconvenience, even from worse to better.
Richard Hooker, English priest and theologian (1554–1600)

•

There is a certain relief in change, even though it be from bad to worse … it is often a comfort to shift one's position and be bruised in a new place.
Tales of a Traveler (1824)
Washington Irving, American writer, historian and diplomat (1783–1859)

•

The issues are the same. We wanted peace on earth, love, and understanding between everyone around the world.
We have learned that change comes slowly.
The Observer (1987)
Sir Paul McCartney, English singer-songwriter and composer (1942–)

•

Plus ça change, plus c'est la même chose. The more things change the more they remain the same.
Les Guêpes (1849)
Alphonse Karr, French critic and writer (1808–1890)

Future shock … the shattering stress and disorientation that we induce in individuals by subjecting them to too much change in too short a time.

Future Shock (1970)

Alvin Toffler, American writer, futurist and businessmen (1928–2016)

CHRISTMAS AND FESTIVE SPIRIT

Still xmas is a good time with all those presents and good food and i hope it will never die out or at any rate not until i am grown up and hav to pay for it all.
How to Be Topp (1954)
Geoffrey Willams (1911–1958) and **Ronald Searle** (1920–2011), English humourists

•

A lovely thing about Christmas is that it's compulsory, like a thunderstorm, and we all go through it together.
Leaving Home (1987)
Garrison Keillor, American writer, humourist and radio personality (1942–)

•

Hogmanay, like all festivals, being but a bank from which we can only draw what we put in.
Sentimental Tommy (1896)
JM Barrie, Scottish writer and dramatist (1860–1937)

•

Now is the accepted time to make your regular annual good resolutions. Next week you can begin paving hell with them as usual.
[Letter to a US newspaper, 1863]
Mark Twain, American writer (1835–1910)

Christmas begins about the first of December with an office party and ends when you finally realise what you spent, around April fifteenth of the next year.
Modern Manners (1983)
PJ O'Rourke, American political satirist and journalist (1947–)

•

Christmas is the time for kindling the fire of hospitality in the hall, the genial flame of charity in the heart.
Old Christmas (1876)
Washington Irving, American writer, historian and diplomat (1783–1859)

•

I will honour Christmas in my heart, and try to keep it all the year. I will live in the Past, the Present, and the Future. The Spirits of all Three shall strive within me. I will not shut out the lessons that they teach!
A Christmas Carol (1843)
Charles Dickens, English writer and social critic (1812–1870)

•

At Christmas I no more desire a rose
Than wish a snow in May's new fangled shows;
But like of each thing that in season grows.
Love's Labour's Lost (1597)
William Shakespeare, English poet and dramatist (1564–1616)

My idea of Christmas, whether old-fashioned or modern, is very simple: loving others. Come to think of it, why do we have to wait for Christmas to do that?

Bob Hope, English-born American comedian and actor (1903–2003)

COMPETITION

If you don't try to win you might as well hold the Olympics in somebody's back yard.
Jesse Owens, American Olympic gold medallist for track and field (1913–1980)

•

The important thing in life is not the victory but the contest; the essential thing is not to have won but to have fought well.
[Speech in London, 1908]
Baron Pierre de Coubertin, French founder of the International Olympic Committee (1863–1937)

•

Know ye not that they which run in a race run all, but one receiveth the prize.
The Bible
Corinthians 9:24

•

Winning is everything. The only ones who remember you when you come second are your wife and your dog.
The Sunday Times (1994)
Damon Hill, British Formula One world champion (1960–)

•

When you are in any contest, you should work as if there were — to the very last minute — a chance to lose it.
[The President's News Conference, 1956]
Dwight D Eisenhower, 34th president of the US (1890–1969)

CONFLICT AND AGGRESSION

War settles nothing ... to win a war is as disastrous as
to lose one!
An Autobiography (1977)
Agatha Christie, English writer (1890–1976)

•

Peace is the only battle worth waging.
Combat (1945)
Albert Camus, French philosopher, writer and journalist (1913–1960)

•

I am not only a pacifist but a militant pacifist. I am willing
to fight for peace. Nothing will end war unless the people
themselves refuse to go to war.
[Interview with George Sylvester Viereck, 1931]
Albert Einstein, German theoretical physicist (1879–1955)

•

The unleashed power of the atom has changed everything save
our modes of thinking, and we thus drift toward unparalleled
catastrophe.
[Telegram to prominent Americans, 1946]
Albert Einstein, German theoretical physicist (1879–1955)

•

There are not fifty ways of fighting, there's only one, and that's to
win. Neither revolution nor war consists in doing what one pleases.
L'Espoir (1937)
André Malraux, French writer (1901–1976)

We are in an armed conflict; that is the phrase I have used.
There has been no declaration of war.
[Speech on the Suez crisis, House of Commons, 1956]
Anthony Eden, prime minister of the UK (1897–1977)

•

Love, friendship, respect do not unite people as much as
common hatred for something.
Notebooks (1921)
Anton Chekhov, Russian writer (1860–1904)

•

If we have no peace, it is because we have forgotten that we
belong to each other.
Mother Teresa, Albanian nun and missionary (1910–1997)

•

After each war there is a little less democracy to save.
Once Around the Sun (1951)
Brooks Atkinson, American theatre critic and writer
(1894–1984)

•

It is not violence that best overcomes hate — nor vengeance
that most certainly heals injury.
Jane Eyre (1847)
Charlotte Brontë, English writer (1816–1855)

First, we are going to cut it off, and then, we are going to kill it.
[Pentagon press briefing on the Gulf War, 1991]
Colin Powell, US general and politician (1937–)

•

It takes in reality only one to make a quarrel. It is useless for the sheep to pass resolutions in favour of vegetarianism, while the wolf remains of a different opinion.
Outspoken Essays: First Series "Patriotism" (1919)
Dean Inge, English writer, priest and educator (1860–1954)

•

A man may build himself a throne of bayonets, but he cannot sit on it.
Philosophy of Plotinus (1923)
Dean Inge, English writer, priest and educator (1860–1954)

•

History is littered with the wars which everybody knew would never happen.
The Times (1967)
Enoch Powell, British politician and scholar (1912–1998)

•

All the war-propaganda, all the screaming and lies and hatred, comes invariably from people who are not fighting.
Homage to Catalonia (1938)
George Orwell, English writer (1903–1950)

The weak have one weapon: the errors of those who think
they are strong.
The Observer (1962)
Georges Bidault, prime minister of France (1899–1983)

•

I renounce war for its consequences, for the lies it lives on
and propagates, for the undying hatred it arouses, for the
dictatorships it puts in the place of democracy, for the starvation
that stalks after it.
[Armistice Day sermon in New York, 1933]
Harry Emerson Fosdick, American pastor (1878–1969)

•

Older men declare war. But it is the youth who must fight
and die.
[Speech in Chicago to the 23rd Republican national convention,
1944]
Herbert Hoover, 31st president of the US (1874–1964)

•

Peace is not made at the council table or by treaties,
but in the hearts of men.
Herbert Hoover, 31st president of the US (1874–1964)

•

Those who in quarrels interpose
Must often wipe a bloody nose.
Fables (1727)
John Gay, English poet (1685–1732)

If the thrill of hunting were in the hunt, or even in the
marksmanship, a camera would do just as well.
Eating Animals (2009)
Jonathan Safran Foer, American writer (1977–)

•

If peace cannot be maintained with honour, it is no longer peace.
[Speech in Greenock, 1853]
Lord John Russell, prime minister of the UK (1792–1878)

•

A war can perhaps be won single-handedly. But peace —
lasting peace — cannot be secured without the support of all.
[Speech to the UN, 2003]
Luiz Inácio Lula da Silva, president of Brazil (1945–)

•

All I have I would have given gladly not to be standing
here today.
[Speech to Congress after the assassination of John F Kennedy,
1963]
Lyndon B Johnson, 36th president of the US (1908–1973)

•

I object to violence because when it appears to do good,
the good is only temporary; the evil it does is permanent.
Mahatma Gandhi, Indian politician, social activist and writer
(1869–1948)

Non-violence is the first article of my faith. It is also the last article of my creed.
[In response to a charge of sedition, 1922]
Mahatma Gandhi, Indian politician, social activist and writer (1869–1948)

•

Weapons are like money; no one knows the meaning of enough.
Einstein's Monsters (1987)
Martin Amis, British writer (1949–)

•

You must not fight too often with one enemy, or you will teach him all your art of war.
Napoleon Bonaparte, French statesman and military leader (1769–1821)

•

It is only a step from the sublime to the ridiculous.
[After the retreat from Moscow, 1812]
Napoleon Bonaparte, French statesman and military leader (1769–1821)

•

It [the Channel] is a mere ditch, and will be crossed as soon as someone has the courage to attempt it.
[Letter to Consul Cambacérès, 1803]
Napoleon Bonaparte, French statesman and military leader (1769–1821)

Wars begin when you will, but they do not end when you please.
Florentine Histories (1532)
Niccolò Machiavelli, Italian diplomat and political philosopher
(1469–1527)

•

The way to win atomic war is to make certain it never starts.
[Speech on Armistice Day, 1948]
Omar Bradley, US general (1893–1981)

•

A man cannot be too careful in the choice of his enemies.
The Picture of Dorian Gray (1891)
Oscar Wilde, Irish dramatist and poet (1854–1900)

•

We hear war called murder. It is not: it is suicide.
The Observer (1930)
Ramsay MacDonald, prime minister of the UK (1866–1937)

•

The brotherhood of man is evoked by particular men according
to their circumstances ... In the name of our freedom and our
brotherhood we are prepared to blow up the other half of
mankind and to be blown up in turn.
The Politics of Experience (1967)
RD Laing, Scottish psychiatrist (1927–1989)

Always remember, others may hate you. Those who hate you
don't win unless you hate them. And then you destroy yourself.
Richard Nixon, 37th president of the US (1913–1994)

•

It is well that war is so terrible. We should grow too fond of it.
[Remark made after the Battle of Fredericksburg, 1862]
Robert E Lee, American commander of the Confederate States
Army (1807–1870)

•

For it's Tommy this, an' Tommy that, an' "Chuck him out,
the brute!" But it's saviour of 'is country when the guns begin
to shoot.
Tommy (1892)
Rudyard Kipling, English journalist and writer (1865–1936)

•

I have never met anyone who wasn't against war.
Even Hitler and Mussolini were, according to themselves.
The New York Times Magazine (1946)
Sir David Low, New Zealand political cartoonist (1891–1963)

•

All the business of war, and indeed all the business of life, is to
endeavour to find out what you don't know by what you do; that's
what I called "guessing what was at the other side of the hill".
Arthur Wellesley, 1st Duke of Wellington, Irish-born British
soldier and statesman (1769–1852)

Red lips are not so red as the stained stones kissed by the
English dead.
Greater Love (1917–1918)
Wilfred Owen, English poet and soldier (1893–1918)

•

My subject is War, and the pity of War. The Poetry is in the pity.
[Draft for a preface, c. 1918]
Wilfred Owen, English poet and soldier (1893–1918)

•

You can't say civilization don't advance, however, for in every war
they kill you in a new way.
The New York Times (1929)
Will Rogers, American actor and humourist (1879–1935)

•

It is a most mistaken way of teaching men to feel they are
brothers, by imbuing their mind with perpetual hatred.
An Enquiry concerning the Principals of Political Justice
William Godwin, English political philosopher and writer
(1756–1836)

•

Those who are at war with others are not at peace with
themselves.
William Hazlitt, English writer and critic (1778–1830)

I gave my life for freedom — This I know:
For those who bade me fight had told me so.
The Souls (1917)
William Norman Ewer, British journalist (1885–1976)

●

Here is the answer which I will give to President Roosevelt ...
Give us the tools and we will finish the job.
[Radio broadcast, 1941]
Sir Winston Churchill, prime minister of the UK, historian and
Nobel Prize winner (1874–1965)

●

It must be a peace without victory ... Only a peace between
equals can last.
[Speech to the US Senate, 1917]
Woodrow Wilson, 28th president of the US (1856–1924)

COURAGE AND DARING

There is no fate that cannot be surmounted by scorn.
The Myth of Sisyphus (1942)
Albert Camus, French philosopher, writer and journalist (1913–1960)

•

Courage is the price that
Life exacts for granting peace.
Courage (1927)
Amelia Earhart, American aviator (1897–disappeared 1937, declared dead 1939)

•

Life shrinks or expands in proportion to one's courage.
The Diary of Anaïs Nin vol. 3 (1941)
Anaïs Nin, French-born Cuban-American writer (1903–1977)

•

Those who have courage to love should have courage to suffer.
The Bertrams (1859)
Anthony Trollope, English writer (1815–1882)

•

True heroism is remarkably sober, very undramatic.
It is not the urge to surpass all others at whatever cost,
but the urge to serve others at whatever cost.
A Hard Road to Glory (1993)
Arthur Ashe, American tennis player and Aids activist (1943–1993)

When I dare to be powerful, to use my strength in the service
of my vision, then it becomes less and less important whether
I am afraid.
The Cancer Journals (1980)
Audre Lorde, American writer and activist (1934–1992)

•

The boy stood on the burning deck, whence all but he had fled;
The flame that lit the battle's wreck shone round him o'er
the dead.
Casabianca (1826)
Felicia Hemans, English poet (1793–1835)

•

A single feat of daring can alter the whole conception of what
is possible.
The Heart of the Matter (1948)
Graham Greene, English writer (1904–1991)

•

Being tactful in audacity is knowing how far one can go too far.
Le Rappel à l'ordre (1926)
Jean Cocteau, French writer and dramatist (1889–1963)

•

Courage is the thing. All goes if courage goes!
[Rectorial address at the University of St Andrews, 1922]
JM Barrie, Scottish writer and dramatist (1860–1937)

Do your duty bravely. Fear God. Honour the King.
[Message to the soldiers of the British Expeditionary Force, 1914]
Lord Kitchener, British soldier and statesman (1850–1916)

•

A coward is incapable of exhibiting love; it is the prerogative
of the brave.
Mahatma Gandhi, Indian politician, social activist and writer
(1869–1948)

•

Valour is stability, not of legs and arms, but of courage
and the soul.
Michel de Montaigne, French philosopher (1533–1592)

•

Ultimately a hero is a man who would argue with the gods,
and so awakens devils to contest his vision.
The Presidential Papers (1963)
Norman Mailer, American writer (1923–2007)

•

I love the man that can smile in trouble, that can gather
strength from distress, and grow brave by reflections.
The American Crisis (1776)
Thomas Paine, English-born political activist, philosopher
and revolutionary (1737–1809)

Bravery never goes out of fashion.
William Makepeace Thackeray, British writer (1811–1863)

•

Courage is rightly esteemed the first of human qualities because as has been said, it is the quality which guarantees all others.
Great Contemporaries (1937)
Sir Winston Churchill, prime minister of the UK, historian and Nobel Prize winner (1874–1965)

CREATIVITY AND THE ARTS

The secret to creativity is knowing how to hide your sources.
Albert Einstein, German theoretical physicist (1879–1955)

•

Discovery consists in seeing what everyone else has seen
and thinking what no one else has thought.
The Scientist Speculates (1962)
Albert Szent-Gyorgyi, Hungarian biochemist (1893–1986)

•

I hate like death the situation of the plagiarist; the glass
I drink from is not large, but at least it is my own.
La Coupe et les Lèvres (1832)
Alfred de Musset, French poet and playwright (1810–1857)

•

When a thing has been said and well said, have no scruple:
take it and copy it.
Anatole France, French poet (1844–1924)

•

Art is a revolt against fate.
Les Voix du silence (1951)
André Malraux, French writer (1901–1976)

•

Cooking is the most ancient of the arts, for Adam was born hungry.
Physiologie du Goût (1825)
Anthelme Brillat-Savarin, French lawyer (1755–1826)

The possession of a book becomes a substitute for reading it.
New York Times Book Review
Anthony Burgess, English writer (1917–1993)

•

The spray can is a tool that can be used for good or ill ...
I always try to leave a wall looking better than I found it.
The Sunday Times (2009)
Banksy, England-based graffiti artist (1974–)

•

I rarely draw what I see — I draw what I feel in my body.
Drawings from a Sculptor's Landscape (1966)
Barbara Hepworth, English sculptor (1903–1975)

•

The function of art is to do more than tell it like it is —
it's to imagine what is possible.
Outlaw Culture (1994)
Bell Hooks, American writer (1952–)

•

Television is simultaneously blamed, often by the same people,
for worsening the world and for being powerless to change it.
Clive James, Australian writer (1939–)

•

It's amazing what you can do with an E in A-level art, twisted
imagination and a chainsaw.
[Acceptance speech for the 1995 Turner Prize]
Damien Hirst, English artist (1965–)

All painting, no matter what you're painting, is abstract in that it's got to be organised.
David Hockney, English artist (1937–)

•

Opera is when a guy gets stabbed in the back and, instead of bleeding, he sings.
Ed Gardner, English conductor (1974–)

•

Another unsettling element in modern art is that common symptom of immaturity, the dread of doing what has been done before.
The Writing of Fiction (1925)
Edith Wharton, American writer (1862–1937)

•

I do not mind what language an opera is sung in so long as it is a language I don't understand.
The Observer (1955)
Edward Appleton, English physicist (1892–1965)

•

The physician can bury his mistakes, but the architect can only advise his client to plant vines — so they should go as far as possible from home to build their first buildings.
Frank Lloyd Wright, American architect (1867–1959)

Feet, why do I need them if I have wings to fly?
[Diary entry that was written after the amputation of her right
leg because of gangrene, 1953]
Frida Kahlo, Mexican painter (1907–1954)

•

Architecture in general is frozen music.
Friedrich von Schelling, German philosopher (1775–1854)

•

Art, like morality, consists of drawing the line somewhere.
GK Chesterton, English writer and critic (1874–1936)

•

The symphony must be like the world. It must embrace
everything.
[Remark to Sibelius, 1907]
Gustav Mahler, Austro-Bohemian composer (1860–1911)

•

You can calculate the worth of a man by the number of his
enemies and the importance of a work of art by the harm
that is spoken of it.
[Letter to Louise Cole, 1853]
Gustave Flaubert, French writer (1821–1880)

•

The artist must be in his work as God is in creation, invisible and
all-powerful; one must sense him everywhere but never see him.
[Letter, 1857]
Gustave Flaubert, French writer (1821–1880)

Life being all inclusion and confusion, and art being all
discrimination and selection.
The Spoils of Poynton (1909)
Henry James, American writer (1843–1916)

·

On stage, I make love to 25,000 people, then I go home alone.
Janis Joplin, American singer (1943–1970)

·

The excellency of every art is its intensity, capable of making
all disagreeables evaporate.
John Keats, English poet (1795–1821)

·

You can't use up creativity. The more you use, the more you have.
Conversations with Maya Angelou (1989)
Maya Angelou, American writer (1928–2014)

·

A film is never really good unless the camera is an eye in the
head of a poet.
Ribbon of Dreams (1958)
Orson Welles, American actor and film director (1915–1985)

·

Every great man nowadays has his disciples, and it is always
Judas who writes the biography.
The Critic as Artist (1891)
Oscar Wilde, Irish dramatist and poet (1854–1900)

Genius does what it must, and talent does what it can.
Owen Meredith, English statesman and poet (1831–1891)

•

Art is not made to decorate rooms. It is an offensive weapon
in the defence against the enemy.
Les Lettres Françaises (1943)
Pablo Picasso, Spanish painter (1881–1973)

•

Treat nature in terms of the cylinder, the sphere, the cone,
all in perspective.
[Letter to Émile Bernard, 1904)
Paul Cézanne, French painter (1839–1906)

•

Architecture is the art of how to waste space.
Philip Johnson, American architect (1906–2005)

•

Fish, to taste good, must swim three times: in water, in butter
and in wine.
Polish proverb

•

Drawing is the true test of art.
Pensées d'Ingres (1922)
JAD Ingres, French painter (1780–1867)

You've got to perform in a role hundreds of times. In keeping it fresh one can become a large, madly humming, demented refrigerator.
New York Herald Tribune (1946)
Sir Ralph Richardson, English actor (1902–1983)

•

Television ... thrives on unreason, and unreason thrives on television ... [It] strikes at the emotions rather than the intellect.
Grand Inquisitor (1989)
Robin Day, British broadcaster (1923–2000)

•

Architecture has its political use; public buildings being the ornament of a country; it establishes a nation, draws people and commerce; makes the people love their native country. Architecture aims at eternity.
Sir Christopher Wren, English architect (1632–1723)

•

In architecture as in all other operative arts, the end must direct the operation. The end is to build well. Well building has three conditions. Commodity, firmness and delight.
Elements of Architecture (1624)
Sir Henry Wotton, English poet and diplomat (1568–1639)

•

Once a month the sky falls on my head, I come to, and I see another movie I want to make.
Time (1998)
Steven Spielberg, American film director and producer (1946–)

Art is the objectification of feeling, and the subjectification of nature.
Mind (1967)
Susanne Langer, American philosopher (1895–1985)

•

I cannot help it that my pictures do not sell. Nevertheless the time will come when people will see that they are worth more than the price of the paint.
[Letter to his brother Theo, 1888]
Vincent van Gogh, Dutch painter (1853–1890)

•

All art constantly aspires towards the condition of music.
Studies in the History of the Renaissance (1873)
Walter Pater, English essayist and critic (1839–1894)

•

No, I ask it for the knowledge of a lifetime.
[Explanation for charging a large fee for a painting completed in two days, 1878]
James McNeill Whistler, American artist (1834–1903)

•

Life is very nice, but it has no shape. It is the purpose of art to give it shape.
The Rehearsal (1950)
Jean Anouilh, French dramatist (1910–1987)

In free society art is not a weapon ... Artists are not engineers of the soul.
[Speech, 1963]
John F Kennedy, 35th president of the US (1917–1963)

•

Fine art is that in which the hand, the head, and the heart of man go together.
John Ruskin, English art critic (1819–1900)

•

Every time I paint a portrait I lose a friend.
John Singer Sargent, American artist (1856–1925)

DEATH AND SORROW

After the first death, there is no other.
A Refusal to Mourn the Death, by Fire, of a Child in London, 1946
Dylan Thomas, Welsh writer (1914–1953)

•

No one ever told me that grief felt so like fear.
A Grief Observed (1961)
CS Lewis, British literary scholar and writer (1898–1963)

•

Time goes, you say? Ah no! Alas, Time stays, we go.
The Paradox of Time (1877)
Henry Austin Dobson, English poet (1840–1921)

•

Death is nothing at all; it does not count. I have only slipped
away into the next room.
[Sermon preached on Whitsunday, 1910]
Henry Scott Holland, English theologian (1847–1918)

•

Sorrow and silence are strong, and patient endurance
is godlike.
Evangeline (1847)
Henry Wadsworth Longfellow, American poet (1807–1882)

The bodies of those that made such a noise and tumult when alive, when dead, lie as quietly among the graves of their neighbours as any others.
Jonathan Edwards, American preacher (1703–1758)

•

I want death to find me planting my cabbages, but caring little for it and even less about the imperfections of my garden.
Michel de Montaigne, French philosopher (1533–1592)

•

Death is no different whined at than withstood.
Aubade (1977)
Philip Larkin, English poet, writer and librarian (1922–1985)

•

However many ways there may be of being alive, it is certain that there are vastly more ways of being dead.
The Blind Watchmaker (1986)
Richard Dawkins, English biologist (1941–)

•

It's a joy to be old.
Kids through school,
The dog dead and the car sold.
A Joy to Be Old (1986)
Roger McGough, English writer, dramatist and broadcaster (1937–)

In this life there's nothing new in dying,
But nor, of course, is living any newer.
Goodbye, My Friend, Goodbye (1925)
Sergei Yesenin, Russian poet (1895–1925)

•

You may my glories and my state depose
But not my griefs;
still am I king of those.
Richard II (1597)
William Shakespeare, English poet and dramatist (1564–1616)

•

If I cannot give consent to my own death, then whose body
is this? Who owns my life?
[Appeal to a Canadian Commons Subcommittee, 1992]
Sue Rodriguez, Canadian euthanasia activist (1951–1994)

•

Many men would take the death-sentence without a whimper
to escape the life-sentence which fate carries in her other hand.
The Mint (1955)
TE Lawrence, British soldier and writer (1888–1935)

•

Life is a great surprise. I do not see why death should not be
an even greater one.
Pale Fire (1962)
Vladimir Nabokov, American-Russian writer (1899–1977)

This is no time for making new enemies.
[On being asked to renounce the Devil on his deathbed]
Voltaire, French writer and philosopher (1694–1778)

•

Nor dread nor hope attend
A dying animal;
A man awaits his end
Dreading and hoping all.
Death (1933)
WB Yeats, Irish poet (1865–1939)

•

When you are old and grey and full of sleep,
And nodding by the fire, take down this book,
And slowly read, and dream of the soft look
Your eyes had once, and of their shadows deep.
When you are Old (1893)
WB Yeats, Irish poet (1865–1939)

•

Men travel faster now, but I do not know if they go
to better things.
Death Comes for the Archbishop (1924)
Willa Cather, American writer (1873–1947)

•

It's not that I'm afraid to die. I just don't want to be there
when it happens.
Death (1975)
Woody Allen, American film director and actor (1935–)

Death ... It's the only thing we haven't succeeded in completely vulgarising.
Aldous Huxley, English writer and philosopher (1894–1963)

•

I mount! I fly!
O Grave! where is thy victory?
O Death! where is thy sting?
The Dying Christian to his Soul (1730)
Alexander Pope, English poet (1688–1744)

•

I am dying with the help of too many physicians.
[Attr.]
Alexander the Great, King of Macedon (356–323 BC)

•

Death has made His darkness beautiful with thee.
In Memoriam AHH (1850)
Alfred, Lord Tennyson, English poet (1809–1892)

•

Hitherto man had to live with the idea of death as an individual; from now onward mankind will have to live with the idea of its death as a species.
[Attr.]
Arthur Koestler, Hungarian-British writer (1905–1983)

After your death you will be what you were before your birth.
Parerga and Paralipomena (1851)
Arthur Schopenhauer, German philosopher (1788–1860)

•

I am become death, the destroyer of worlds.
Bhagavad Gita
Quoted by J Robert Oppenheimer after testing the first atomic
bomb in 1945

•

What argufies pride and ambition?
Soon or late death will take us in tow:
Each bullet has got its commission,
And when our time's come we must go.
A Sailor's Philosophy
Charles Dibdin, British composer (1745–1814)

•

He had been, he said, a most unconscionable time dying;
but he hoped that they would excuse it.
Charles II, King of England, Scotland and Ireland (1630–1685)

•

Though they go mad they shall be sane,
Though they sink through the sea they shall rise again;
Though lovers be lost love shall not;
And death shall have no dominion.
And Death Shall Have No Dominion (1936)
Dylan Thomas, Welsh writer (1914–1953)

ECONOMICS AND COMMERCE

It is not from the benevolence of the butcher, the brewer, or the baker, that we expect our dinner, but from their regard to their own interest. We address ourselves not to their humanity but to their self love.
Wealth of Nations (1776)
Adam Smith, Scottish philosopher and economist (1723–1790)

•

An infectious greed seemed to grip much of our business community.
[Addressing the Senate banking committee in 2002, summing up the late 1990s]
Alan Greenspan, American economist (1926–)

•

No permanent elevation of a people can be effected without commerce.
Quarterly Review (1861)
David Livingstone, Scottish missionary and explorer (1813–1873)

•

If you want people motivated to do a good job, give them a good job to do.
Industry Week (1987)
Frederick Herzberg, American psychologist (1923–2000)

[Commercialism is] doing well that which should not be done at all.
The Listener (1975)
Gore Vidal, American writer (1925–2012)

•

In a consumer society there are inevitably two kinds of slaves: the prisoners of addiction and the prisoners of envy.
Ivan Illich, Croatian-Austrian philosopher (1926–2002)

•

Trickle-down theory — the less than elegant metaphor that if one feeds the horse enough oats, some will pass through to the road for the sparrows.
JK Galbraith, Canadian economist (1908–2006)

•

When buying and selling are controlled by legislation, the first things to be bought and sold are legislators.
PJ O'Rourke, American political satirist and journalist (1947–)

•

In the first stone which he (the savage) flings at the wild animal he pursues, in the first stick that he seizes to strike down the fruit which hangs above his reach, we see the appropriation of one article for the purpose of aiding in the acquisition of another and thus we discover the origin of capital.
An Essay on the Production of Wealth (1821)
Robert Torrens, British economist (1780–1864)

Excise: a hateful tax levied upon commodities.
A Dictionary of the English Language (1755)
Samuel Johnson, English writer, critic and lexicographer
(1709–1784)

•

A budget is a financial schedule adopted to prevent part
of the month being left at the end of your money.
Unknown

•

Finance is, as it were, the stomach of the country, from which
all the other organs take their tone.
WE Gladstone, prime minister of the UK (1809–1898)

•

People of the same trade seldom meet together, even for
merriment and diversion, but the conversation ends in a
conspiracy against the public, or in some contrivance to raise
prices.
Wealth of Nations (1776)
Adam Smith, Scottish philosopher and economist (1723–1790)

•

Nothing is illegal if one hundred businessmen decide to do it.
[Attr.]
Andrew Young, US Ambassador to the United Nations (1932–)

Being good in business is the most fascinating kind of art.
The Observer (1987)
Andy Warhol, American artist (1928–1987)

•

I am still looking for the modern equivalent of those Quakers
who ran successful businesses, made money because they
offered honest products and treated their people decently …
This business creed, sadly, seems long forgotten.
Body and Soul (1991)
Anita Roddick, British businesswoman (1942–2007)

•

A Company for carrying on an undertaking of Great Advantage,
but no one to know what it is.
The South Sea Company Prospectus (1711)

•

The secret of business is to know something that nobody
else knows.
Aristotle Onassis, Greek shipping magnate (1906–1975)

•

No nation was ever ruined by trade.
Benjamin Franklin, founding father of the US (1706–1790)

•

It takes one hen to lay an egg, But seven men to sell it.
The Regimental Hen
CJ Dennis, Australian poet (1876–1938)

The business of America is business.
[Speech, 1925]
Calvin Coolidge, 30th president of the US (1872–1933)

·

In the factory we make cosmetics. In the store we sell hope.
Charles Revson, American businessman who founded
Revlon Cosmetics (1906–1975)

·

Did you ever expect a corporation to have a conscience,
when it has no soul to be damned, and no body to be
kicked?
Edward Thurlow, 1st Baron, lord chancellor (1731–1806)

·

The business man, in fact, acquiesces in this assumption
of his inferiority, even when he protests against it. He is the
only man who is forever apologising for his occupation.
Prejudices (1927)
HL Mencken, American journalist and satirist (1880–1956)

·

A business that makes nothing but money is a poor kind
of business.
Henry Ford, American industrialist and businessman
(1863–1947)

Generous people make bad shopkeepers.
Illusions perdues (1843)
Honoré de Balzac, French writer (1799–1850)

•

The big print giveth and the fine print taketh away.
[Attr.]
J Fulton Sheen, American theologian (1895–1979)

EDUCATION

To the uneducated, an A is just three sticks.
AA Milne, English writer (1882–1956)

•

Great and good is the typical Don, and of evil and wrong the foe,
Good and great, I'm a Don myself, and therefore I ought to know.
The Megalopsychiad (1904)
AD Godley, English writer (1856–1925)

•

Men must be taught as if you taught them not, and things
unknown proposed as things forgot.
An Essay on Criticism (1711)
Alexander Pope, English poet (1688–1744)

•

You are as many people as languages you know.
Armenian proverb

•

Upon the education of the people of this country the fate
of this country depends.
Benjamin Disraeli, prime minister of the UK (1804–1881)

To be conscious that you are ignorant is a great step to knowledge.
Sybil (1845)
Benjamin Disraeli, prime minister of the UK (1804–1881)

•

Tell me and I forget, teach me and I may remember, involve me and I learn.
Benjamin Franklin, founding father of the US (1706–1790)

•

The task of the modern educator is not to cut down jungles, but to irrigate deserts.
CS Lewis, British literary scholar and writer (1898–1963)

•

If there is anything that we wish to change in the child we should first examine it and see whether it is not something that could better be changed in ourselves.
Carl Jung, Swiss psychologist (1875–1961)

•

Examinations are formidable even to the best prepared, for the greatest fool may ask more than the wisest man can answer.
Charles Caleb Colton, English cleric (1780–1832)

•

No matter how busy you may think you are, you must find time for reading, or surrender yourself to self-chosen ignorance.
Confucius, Chinese teacher (551–479 BC)

Even when walking in the company of two other men, I am bound to be able to learn from them. The good points of one I copy; the bad points of the other I correct in myself.
The Analects (AD 206–220)
Confucius, Chinese teacher (551–479 BC)

•

Conversation enriches the understanding, but solitude is the school of genius.
Edward Gibbon, English historian (1737–1784)

•

Great education must ultimately be limited to one who insists on knowing, the rest is mere sheep herding.
The ABC of Reading (1834)
Ezra Pound, American poet (1885–1972)

•

We may not be able to prepare the future for our children, but we can at least prepare our children for the future.
Franklin D Roosevelt, 32nd president of the US (1882–1945)

•

It [education] has produced a vast population able to read but unable to distinguish what is worth reading, an easy prey to sensations and cheap appeals.
English Social History (1942)
GM Trevelyan, British historian (1876–1962)

A teacher affects eternity; he can never tell where his influence stops.
Henry Adams, American historian (1838–1918)

•

As we read the school reports on our children we realise a sense of relief that … nobody is reporting in this fashion on us!
Reader's Digest (1964)
JB Priestley, English writer, dramatist and critic (1894–1984)

•

To live for a time close to great minds is the best kind of education.
Memory Hold-the-Door (1940)
John Buchan, Scottish writer, historian and politician (1875–1940)

•

We must beat the iron while it is hot, but we may polish it at leisure.
John Dryden, English poet (1631–1700)

•

To make your children capable of honesty is the beginning of education.
John Ruskin, English art critic (1819–1900)

•

One child, one teacher, one book and one pen can change the world. Education is the only solution. Education first.
Malala Yousafzai, Pakistani activist and Nobel Prize winner (1997–)

If you want to know the reason why I'm standing here,
it's because of education. I never cut class.
[Speech to schoolgirls in London, 2009]
Michelle Obama, first lady of the US (1964–)

•

To me education is a leading out of what is already there in
the pupil's soul. To Miss Mackay it is a putting in of something
that is not there, and that is not what I call education.
I call it intrusion.
The Prime of Miss Jean Brodie (1961)
Muriel Spark, Scottish writer (1918–2006)

•

You've got to be taught before it's too late
Before you are six or seven or eight
To hate all the people your relatives hate
You've got to be carefully taught.
You've Got to Be Carefully Taught, from *South Pacific* (1949)
Richard Rodgers, American composer (1902–1979) and
Oscar Hammerstein II, American lyricist (1895–1960)

•

Education is the ability to listen to almost anything without
losing your temper or your self-confidence.
Reader's Digest (1960)
Robert Frost, American poet (1874–1963)

Try to learn something about everything and everything about something.
[Memorial stone]
TH Huxley, English biologist (1825–1895)

•

For every person who wants to teach there are approximately thirty who don't want to learn — much.
And Now All This (1932)
WC Sellar (1898–1951) and **RJ Yeatman** (1898–1968), British writers

•

Education is what most people receive, many pass on and few actually have.
Pro domo et mundo (1912)
Karl Kraus, Austrian writer (1874–1936)

•

Education makes a people easy to lead, but difficult to drive; easy to govern, but impossible to enslave.
[Attr.]
Henry Brougham, 1st Baron Brougham and Vaux, lord chancellor (1778–1868)

EMOTIONS

Jealousy is all the fun you think they had.
Fear of Flying (1973)
Erica Jong, American writer (1942–)

•

A little alarm now and then keeps life from stagnation.
Camilla (1796)
Fanny Burney, English writer and diarist (1752–1840)

•

Human feeling is like the mighty rivers that bless the earth:
it does not wait for beauty — it flows with resistless force and
brings beauty with it.
Adam Bede (1859)
George Eliot, English writer (1819–1880)

•

Guilt feelings so often arise from accusations rather than
from crimes.
The Sea, The Sea (1978)
Iris Murdoch, Irish writer (1919–1999)

•

It is in man's heart that the life of nature's spectacle exists;
to see it, one must feel it.
Emile (1762)
Jean-Jacques Rousseau, Genevan philosopher (1712–1778)

It is very difficult to get up resentment towards persons whom one has never seen.
John Henry Newman, English poet and cardinal (1801–1890)

•

Hatred is a feeling which leads to the extinction of values.
Meditations on Quixote (1914)
José Ortega y Gasset, Spanish philosopher (1883–1955)

•

Indeed, revenge is always the pleasure of a paltry, feeble, tiny mind.
Satires
Juvenal, Roman poet (47–?)

•

The threshold of a new house is a lonely place.
The Handmaid's Tale (1985)
Margaret Atwood, Canadian writer (1939–)

•

Man is the only animal that blushes. Or needs to.
Following the Equator (1897)
Mark Twain, American writer (1835–1910)

•

Sentimentality is the emotional promiscuity of those who have no sentiment.
Cannibals and Christians (1966)
Norman Mailer, American writer (1923–2007)

As we all know from witnessing the consuming jealousy of husbands who are never faithful, people do not confine themselves to the emotions to which they are entitled.
The Naked Civil Servant (1968)
Quentin Crisp, English writer, raconteur and actor (1908–1999)

•

True guilt is guilt at the obligation one owes to oneself to be oneself. False guilt is guilt felt at not being what other people feel one ought to be or assume that one is.
Self and Others (1961)
RD Laing, Scottish psychiatrist (1927–1989)

•

Madness need not be all breakdown. It may also be break-through.
The Politics of Experience (1967)
RD Laing, Scottish psychiatrist (1927–1989)

•

I know a man that had this trick of melancholy sold a goodly manor for a song.
All's Well that Ends Well (1603–4)
William Shakespeare, English poet and dramatist (1564–1616)

EXPERIENCE AND AGE

The house of delusions is cheap to build but drafty to live in.
AE Housman, English poet (1859–1936)

·

Nothing is inevitable until it happens.
AJP Taylor, English historian (1906–1990)

·

What you see in yourself is what you see in the world.
Afghan proverb

·

What we learn in a time of pestilence: that there are more things
to admire in men than to despise.
The Plague (1947)
Albert Camus, French philosopher, writer and journalist (1913–
1960)

·

Every revolutionary ends as an oppressor or a heretic.
The Rebel (1951)
Albert Camus, French philosopher, writer and journalist (1913–
1960)

·

The eternal mystery of the world is its comprehensibility ...
The fact that it is comprehensible is a miracle.
Albert Einstein, German theoretical physicist (1879–1955)

I am a part of all that I have met.
Ulysses (1842)
Alfred, Lord Tennyson, English poet (1809–1892)

•

The more one gets to know of men, the more one values dogs.
L'esprit des bêtes (1847)
Alphonse Toussenel, French writer (1803–1885)

•

How seldom is it that theories stand the wear and tear
of practice!
Thackeray (1879)
Anthony Trollope, English writer (1815–1882)

•

It has been my experience that one cannot, in any shape or form,
depend on human relations for lasting reward. It is only work
that truly satisfies.
The Lonely Life (1962)
Bette Davis, American actress (1908–1989)

•

I don't like people who have never fallen or stumbled.
Their virtue is lifeless and it isn't of much value.
Life hasn't revealed its beauty to them.
Doctor Zhivago (1958)
Boris Pasternak, Russian poet (1890–1960)

Success makes life easier. It doesn't make living easier.
Q magazine (1992)
Bruce Springsteen, American rock singer and songwriter (1949–)

•

Hardship often prepares an ordinary person for an
extraordinary destiny.
CS Lewis, British literary scholar and writer (1898–1963)

•

Some day you will be old enough to start reading
fairy tales again.
CS Lewis, British literary scholar and writer (1898–1963)

•

Custom reconciles us to everything.
Edmund Burke, Irish philosopher and statesman (1729–1797)

•

To rectify past blunders is impossible, but we might profit
by the experience of them.
George Washington, 1st president of the US (1722–1799)

•

We do not know the true value of our moments until they have
undergone the test of memory.
Georges Duhamel, French writer (1884–1966)

The more acute the experience, the less articulate its expression.
Harold Pinter, British playwright (1930–2008)

•

If only youth knew, if only age could.
Les Prémices (1594)
Henri Estienne, French printer (1528–1598)

•

Nothing ever becomes real till it is experienced; even a proverb
is no proverb to you till your life has illustrated it.
John Keats, English poet (1795–1821)

•

No man was ever so completely skilled in the conduct of life,
as not to receive new information from age and experience.
Jonathan Swift, Irish poet and satirist (1667–1745)

•

Every man desires to live long; but no man would be old.
Thoughts on Various Subjects (1727)
Jonathan Swift, Irish poet and satirist (1667–1745)

•

As Ovid has sweetly in parable told,
We harden like trees, and like rivers grow cold.
Lady Mary Wortley Montagu, English writer (1689–1762)

I think your whole life shows in your face and you should
be proud of that.
[Interview in *The Daily Telegraph*, 1988]
Lauren Bacall, American actress (1924–2014)

•

Everything's got a moral, if you can only find it.
Alice's Adventures in Wonderland (1865)
Lewis Carroll, English writer (1832–1898)

•

Experience is the name everyone gives to their mistakes.
Lady Windermere's Fan (1892)
Oscar Wilde, Irish dramatist and poet (1854–1900)

•

Whatever strengthens and purifies the affections, enlarges
the imagination, and adds spirit to sense, is useful.
Percy Bysshe Shelley, English poet (1792–1822)

•

Personally I'm always ready to learn, although I do not always
like being taught.
Sir Winston Churchill, prime minister of the UK, historian and
Nobel Prize winner (1874–1965)

•

There are some things you learn best in calm, and some in storm.
The Song of the Lark (1915)
Willa Cather, American writer (1873–1947)

Experience is not what happens to a man. It is what a man does with what happens to him.
[Attr.]
Aldous Huxley, English writer and philosopher (1894–1963)

•

You should make a point of trying every experience once, excepting incest and folk dancing.
Farewell My Youth (1943)
Arnold Bax, English composer (1833–1953)

•

Experience keeps a dear school, but fools will learn in no other.
Poor Richard's Almanac (1743)
Benjamin Franklin, founding father of the US (1706–1790)

•

Experience teaches you that the man who looks you straight in the eye, particularly if he adds a firm handshake, is hiding something.
Enter, Conversing (1962)
Clifton Fadiman, American intellectual (1904–1999)

•

An optimist is a guy that has never had much experience.
Archy and Mehitabel (1927)
Don Marquis, American humourist (1878–1937)

Experience isn't interesting till it begins to repeat itself —
in fact, till it does that, it hardly is experience.
The Death of the Heart (1938)
Elizabeth Bowen, Irish writer (1899–1973)

•

The man who views the world at fifty the same as he did at
twenty has wasted thirty years of his life.
Playboy (1975)
Muhammad Ali, American professional boxer (1942–2016)

FREEDOM AND TOLERANCE

Freedom is not choosing; that is merely the move that we make when all is already lost. Freedom is knowing and understanding and respecting things quite other than ourselves.
The Sublime and the Beautiful Revisited (1959)
Iris Murdoch, Irish writer (1919–1999)

•

I disapprove of what you say, but I will defend to the death your right to say it.
Voltaire, French writer and philosopher (1694–1778)

•

Englishmen never will be slaves: they are free to do whatever the government and public opinion allow them to do.
George Bernard Shaw, Irish playwright (1856–1950)

•

Liberty means responsibility. That is why most men dread it.
Man and Superman (1903)
George Bernard Shaw, Irish playwright (1856–1950)

•

Freedom is the freedom to say that two plus two make four. If that is granted, all else follows.
Nineteen Eighty-Four (1949)
George Orwell, English writer (1903–1950)

Where they burn books, they will also ultimately burn people.
Almansor: A Tragedy (1823)
Heinrich Heine, German poet (1797–1856)

•

Was there ever in anyone's life span a point free in time, devoid
of memory, a night when choice was any more than the sum of
all the choices gone before?
Run River (1963)
Joan Didion, American journalist (1934–)

•

The condition upon which God hath given liberty to man
is eternal vigilance; which condition if he break, servitude
is at once the consequence of his crime, and the punishment
of his guilt.
[Speech, 1790]
John Philpot Curran, Irish orator (1750–1817)

•

The moment a slave resolves that he will no longer be a slave,
his fetters fall. He frees himself and shows the way to others.
Freedom and slavery are mental states.
Mahatma Gandhi, Indian politician, social activist and writer
(1869–1948)

•

It is by the goodness of God that in our country we have those
three unspeakably precious things: freedom of speech, freedom
of conscience, and the prudence never to practise either of them.
Following the Equator (1897)
Mark Twain, American writer (1835–1910)

A man able to think isn't defeated — even when he is defeated.
The Sunday Times (1984)
Milan Kundera, Czech-French writer (1929–)

•

Censorship is never over for those who have experienced it.
[Lecture, 1990]
Nadine Gordimer, South African writer (1923–2014)

•

If we don't believe in freedom of expression for people
we despise, we don't believe in it at all.
Noam Chomsky, American linguist and philosopher (1928–)

•

I know not what course others may take; but as for me,
give me liberty, or give me death.
Patrick Henry, governor of Virginia (1736–1799)

•

Perfect freedom is reserved for the man who lives by his own
work and in that work does what he wants to do.
Speculum Mentis (1924)
RG Collingwood, English philosopher (1889–1943)

•

People always say that I didn't give up my seat because I was
tired, but that isn't true. No, the only tired I was, was tired of
giving in.
Rosa Parks, American activist (1913–2005)

The boisterous sea of liberty is never without a wave.
Thomas Jefferson, 3rd president of the US (1743–1826)

•

Happiness depends on being free, and freedom depends
on being courageous.
History of the Peloponnesian War
Thucydides, Athenian historian (460–395 BC)

•

The love of liberty is the love of others. The love of power
is the love of ourselves.
Political Essays (1819)
William Hazlitt, English writer and critic (1778–1830)

•

The enemies of freedom do not argue; they shout and
they shoot.
William Ralph Inge, English writer (1860–1954)

•

I cannot and will not give any undertaking at a time when I,
and you, the people, are not free. Your freedom and mine cannot
be separated.
[Message to a rally in Soweto, 1985]
Nelson Mandela, president of South Africa (1918–2013)

Stone walls do not a prison make
Nor iron bars a cage;
Minds innocent and quiet take
That for an hermitage;
If I have freedom in my love,
And in my soul am free;
Angels alone, that soar above,
Enjoy such liberty.
To Althea, From Prison (1649)
Richard Lovelace, English poet (1617–1657)

•

The tree of liberty must be refreshed from time to time with the blood of patriots and tyrants. It is its natural manure.
[Letter to WS Smith, 1787]
Thomas Jefferson, 3rd president of the US (1743–1826)

•

So long as the state exists there is no freedom. When there is freedom there will be no state.
The State and Revolution (1917)
VI Lenin, Russian revolutionary (1870–1924)

•

Liberty was born in England from the quarrels of tyrants.
Lettres philosophiques (1734)
Voltaire, French writer and philosopher (1694–1778)

FRIENDSHIP

Think where man's glory most begins and ends
And say my glory was I had such friends.
The Municipal Gallery Revisited (1939)
WB Yeats, Irish poet (1865–1939)

•

Friendship is the only cement that will ever hold the
world together.
Woodrow Wilson, 28th president of the US (1856–1924)

•

If a man does not make new acquaintance as he advances
through life, he will soon find himself left alone. A man,
Sir, should keep his friendship in constant repair.
Samuel Johnson, English writer, critic and lexicographer
(1709–1784)

•

Go often to the house of a friend, for weeds soon choke up
the unused path.
Scandinavian proverb

•

Be slow in choosing a friend, but slower in changing him.
Scottish proverb

Relations are made by fate, friends by choice.
Malheur et pitié (1803)
Abbé Jacques Delille, French poet (1738–1813)

•

There are no true friends in politics. We are all sharks circling
and waiting, for traces of blood to appear in the water.
[Diary, 1990]
Alan Clark, British member of parliament (1928–1999)

•

True friendship's laws are by this rule express'd,
Welcome the coming, speed the parting guest.
[In his translation of Homer's *Odyssey*, 1726]
Alexander Pope, English poet (1688–1744)

•

Antipathy: The sentiment inspired by one's friend's friend.
The Enlarged Devil's Dictionary (1961)
Ambrose Bierce, American writer (1842–1914)

•

A faithful friend is a sturdy shelter: he that has found one has
found a treasure. There is nothing so precious as a faithful
friend, and no scales can measure his excellence.
Apocrypha, Ecclesiasticus

A single soul dwelling in two bodies.
Lives of Philosophers (c. AD 200), Diogenes Laërtius
[On being asked what a friend was]
Aristotle, ancient Greek philosopher and scientist (384–322 BC)

•

Friendship is unnecessary, like philosophy, like art ...
It has no survival value; rather it is one of those things that
give value to survival.
The Four Loves (c. 1936)
CS Lewis, British literary scholar and writer (1898–1963)

•

Friendship often ends in love; but love in friendship – never.
Lacon (1820)
Charles Caleb Colton, English cleric (1780–1832)

•

The shifts of fortune test the reliability of friends.
Cicero, Roman statesman (106–43 BC)

•

My true friends have always given me that supreme proof
of devotion, a spontaneous aversion for the man I loved.
Colette, French writer (1873–1954)

•

We read that we ought to forgive our enemies; but we do not
read that we ought to forgive our friends.
Cosimo de' Medici, Italian banker (1389–1464)

We cherish our friends not for their ability to amuse us,
but for our ability to amuse them.
Evelyn Waugh, English writer, journalist and book reviewer
(1903–1966)

•

It is the worst solitude, to have no true friendships.
The Advancement of Learning (1605)
Francis Bacon, English philosopher, statesman and essayist
(1561–1626)

•

Give me the avowed, erect and manly foe;
Firm I can meet, perhaps return the blow;
But of all plagues, good heaven, thy wrath can send,
Save me, oh, save me, from the candid friend.
New Morality (1821)
George Canning, prime minister of the UK (1770–1827)

•

Whenever a friend succeeds, a little something in me dies.
The Sunday Times Magazine (1973)
Gore Vidal, American writer (1925–2012)

•

One friend in a lifetime is much; two are many; three are
hardly possible. Friendship needs a certain parallelism of life,
a community of thought, a rivalry of aim.
The Education of Henry Adams (1918)
Henry Adams, American historian (1838–1918)

From quiet homes and first beginning,
Out to the undiscovered ends,
There's nothing worth the wear of winning,
But laughter and the love of friends.
Verses (1910)
Hilaire Belloc, Anglo-French writer (1870–1953)

•

Friends are God's apology for relations.
God's Apology (1977)
Hugh Kingsmill, British journalist (1889–1949)

•

Think where man's glory most begins and ends,
And say my glory was I had such friends.
The Municipal Gallery Revisited (1937)
WB Yeats, Irish poet (1865–1939)

•

I no doubt deserved my enemies, but I don't believe I deserved
my friends.
Biography and the Human Heart (1932)
Walt Whitman, American poet (1819–1892)

•

Friendship is constant in all other things
Save in the office and affairs of love.
Much Ado About Nothing (1598–99)
William Shakespeare, English poet and dramatist (1564–1616)

An open foe may prove a curse,
But a pretended friend is worse.
Fables (1727)
John Gay, English poet (1685–1732)

·

We make our friends, we make our enemies; but God makes our next-door neighbour.
Heretics (1905)
GK Chesterton, English writer and critic (1874–1936)

FUN AND HUMOUR

As we journey through life, discarding baggage along the way, we should keep an iron grip, to the very end, on the capacity for silliness. It preserves the soul from desiccation.
Humphrey Lyttelton, English jazz musician (1921–2008)

•

Time spent laughing is time spent with the gods.
Japanese proverb

•

Always laugh when you can. It is cheap medicine.
George Gordon, **Lord Byron**, English nobleman and poet (1788–1824)

•

Good taste and humour … are a contradiction in terms, like a chaste whore.
Time (1953)
Malcolm Muggeridge, British journalist (1903–1990)

•

Comedy is simply a funny way of being serious.
Peter Ustinov, English actor, director and writer (1921–2004)

The marvellous thing about a joke with a double meaning
is that it can only mean one thing.
[Attr.]
Ronnie Barker, English actor (1929–2005)

•

Everything is funny as long as it is happening to someone else.
The Illiterate Digest (1924)
Will Rogers, American actor and humourist (1879–1935)

•

Nothing is so impenetrable as laughter in a language you
don't understand.
An Egyptian Journal (1985)
William Golding, British writer (1911–1993)

•

I make myself laugh at everything, for fear of having to cry.
Le Barbier de Seville (1775)
Beaumarchais, French polymath and playwright (1732–1799)

•

It's a good deed to forget a poor joke.
The Observer (1943)
Brendan Bracken, Irish businessman and wartime government
minister (1901–1958)

•

A joke's a very serious thing.
The Ghost (1763)
Charles Churchill, English poet (1731–1764)

Laugh and the world laughs with you;
Weep, and you weep alone;
For the sad old earth must borrow its mirth,
But has trouble enough of its own.
Solitude (1917)
Ella Wheeler Wilcox, American writer and poet (1850–1919)

•

Men will confess to treason, murder, arson, false teeth, or a wig.
How many of them will own up to a lack of humour?
Colby Essays (1926)
Frank Moore Colby, American writer (1865–1925)

•

My way of joking is to tell the truth. It's the funniest joke
in the world.
John Bull's Other Island (1907)
George Bernard Shaw, Irish playwright (1856–1950)

•

A difference of taste in jokes is a great strain on the affections.
Daniel Deronda (1876)
George Eliot, English writer (1819–1880)

•

I love such mirth as does not make friends ashamed to look
upon one another next morning.
The Compleat Angler (1653)
Izaak Walton, English writer (1593–1683)

GOOD AND BAD

What we call evil is simply ignorance bumping its head
in the dark.
[Attr.]
Henry Ford, American industrialist and businessman (1863–1947)

•

Mostly, we are good when it makes sense. A good society is one
that makes sense of being good.
Ian McEwan, English writer (1948–)

•

Nothing in the world — indeed nothing even beyond the world
— can possibly be conceived which could be called good without
qualification except a good will.
Foundation of the Metaphysics of Morals (1785)
Immanuel Kant, German philosopher (1724–1804)

•

Being cruel to be kind is just ordinary cruelty with an excuse
made for it.
Daughters and Sons (1937)
Ivy Compton-Burnett, English writer (1884–1969)

•

Good, the more communicated, more abundant grows.
Paradise Lost, Book V (1667)
John Milton, English poet (1608–1674)

The belief in a supernatural source of evil is not necessary;
men alone are quite capable of every wickedness.
Under Western Eyes (1911)
Joseph Conrad, Polish-British writer (1857–1924)

•

There is a crack in everything. That's how the light gets in.
Leonard Cohen, Canadian singer-songwriter (1934–2016)

•

To be good is noble; but to show others how to be good is nobler
and no trouble.
Mark Twain, American writer (1835–1910)

•

For it is in the most polished society that noisome reptiles
and venomous serpents lurk under the rank herbage.
A Vindication of the Rights of Woman (1792)
Mary Wollstonecraft, English writer (1759–1797)

•

Imaginary evil is romantic and varied; real evil is gloomy,
monotonous, barren, boring. Imaginary good is boring;
real good is always new, marvellous, intoxicating.
Gravity and Grace (1947)
Simone Weil, French philosopher (1909–1943)

•

Better is the enemy of good.
Voltaire, French writer and philosopher (1694–1778)

If a thing be really good, it can be shown to be such.
William Godwin, English political philosopher and writer
(1756–1836)

•

You spotted snakes with double tongue,
Thorny hedgehogs, be not seen;
Newts, and blind-worms, do no wrong;
Come not near our fairy queen.
A Midsummer Night's Dream (1605)
William Shakespeare, English poet and dramatist (1564–1616)

•

Whatever is the first time persons hear evil, it is quite certain
that good has been beforehand with them, and they have a
something within them which tells them it is evil.
Parochial and Plain Sermons (1839)
John Henry Newman, English poet and cardinal (1801–1890)

•

There is scarcely a single man clever enough to know
all the evil he does.
Maximes (1678)
François de La Rochefoucauld, French writer (1613–1680)

•

Whenever I'm caught between two evils, I take the one
I've never tried.
Klondike Annie (1936)
Mae West, American actress (1893–1980)

If someone tells you he is going to make "a realistic decision"
you immediately understand that he has resolved to do
something bad.
On the Contrary (1961)
Mary McCarthy, American writer (1912–1989)

•

What is the greatest good and evil? — two ends of an invisible
chain which come closer together the further they move apart.
Vadim (1834)
Mikhail Lermontov, Russian writer (1814–1841)

•

The fear of one evil often leads us into a greater one.
L'Art Poétique (1674)
Nicolas Boileau-Despréaux, French poet (1636–1711)

•

Don't let us make imaginary evils, when you know we have
so many real ones to encounter.
The Good Natur'd Man (1768)
Oliver Goldsmith, Irish writer and dramatist (1728–1774)

•

We must touch his weaknesses with a delicate hand.
There are some faults so nearly allied to excellence, that
we can scarce weed out the vice without eradicating the virtue.
The Good Natur'd Man (1768)
Oliver Goldsmith, Irish writer and dramatist (1728–1774)

We are each our own devil, and we make this world our hell.

The Duchess of Padua (1883)

Oscar Wilde, Irish dramatist and poet (1854–1900)

GOVERNANCE AND SOCIETY

You only have power over people so long as you don't
take everything away from them. But when you've robbed
a man of everything, he's no longer in your power —
he's free again.
In the First Circle (1968)
Alexander Solzhenitsyn, Russian writer (1918–2008)

•

In the service of the people we followed such a policy
that socialism would not lose its human face.
[Communist Party newspaper *Rudé Právo*, 1968]
Alexander Dubcek, Czechoslovak statesman (1921–1992)

•

The thoughts of a prisoner — they're not free either.
They keep returning to the same things.
One Day in the Life of Ivan Denisovich (1962)
Alexander Solzhenitsyn, Russian writer (1918–2008)

•

Had I been present at the Creation, I would have given
some useful hints for the better ordering of the universe.
Alfonso, King of Castile (1221–84)

Although I am not myself a devotee of bigness for bigness' sake, I would rather be kept alive in the efficient if cold altruism of a large hospital than expire in a gush of warm sympathy in a small one.
[House of Commons, 1946]
Aneurin Bevan, Secretary of State for Health of the UK (1897–1960)

．

You must trust and believe in people or life becomes impossible.
Anton Chekhov, Russian writer (1860–1904)

．

The car, the furniture, the wife, the children — everything has to be disposable. Because you see the main thing today is — shopping.
The Price (1968)
Arthur Miller, American playwright (1915–2005)

．

"Change" is scientific, "progress" is ethical; change is indubitable, whereas progress is a matter of controversy.
Bertrand Russell, British philosopher, mathematician, historian and writer (1872–1970)

．

It is preoccupation with possessions, more than anything else, that prevents us from living freely and nobly.
Bertrand Russell, British philosopher, mathematician, historian and writer (1872–1970)

No nation was ever so virtuous as each believes itself, and none was ever so wicked as each believes the other.
Justice in War-Time (1916)
Bertrand Russell, British philosopher, mathematician, historian and writer (1872–1970)

•

We used to build civilisations. Now we build shopping malls.
Neither Here Nor There (1991)
Bill Bryson, American writer (1952–)

•

When you think of the long and gloomy history of man, you will find more hideous crimes have been committed in the name of obedience than have ever been committed in the name of rebellion.
CP Snow, English writer (1905–1980)

•

Justice extorts no reward, no kind of price; she is sought, therefore, for her own sake.
Cicero, Roman statesman (106–43 BC)

•

Democracy means government by discussion, but it is only effective if you can stop people talking.
[Speech at Oxford, 1957]
Clement Attlee, prime minister of the UK (1883–1967)

Slums may well be breeding-grounds of crime, but middle-class suburbs are incubators of apathy and delirium.
The Unquiet Grave (1944)
Cyril Connolly, English writer and literary critic (1903–1974)

•

Death is the most convenient time to tax rich people.
David Lloyd George, prime minister of the UK (1863–1945)

•

Anarchism is founded on the observation that since few men are wise enough to rule themselves, even fewer are wise enough to rule others.
A Voice Crying in the Wilderness (1989)
Edward Abbey, American writer (1927–1989)

•

In the case of nutrition and health, just as in the case of education, the gentleman in Whitehall really does know better what is good for people than the people know themselves.
The Socialist Case (1947)
Douglas Jay, British politician (1907–1996)

•

The whole world is in revolt. Soon there will be only five kings left — the King of England, the King of Spades, the King of Clubs, the King of Hearts and the King of Diamonds.
Farouk, King of Egypt (1920–1965)

These unhappy times call for the building of plans that ... build
from the bottom up and not from the top down, that put their
faith once more in the forgotten man at the bottom of the
economic pyramid.
[Radio address, 1932]
Franklin D Roosevelt, 32nd president of the US (1882–1945)

•

I come from suburbia ... and I don't ever want to go back.
It's the one place in the world that's further away than
anywhere else.
The Glittering Prizes (1976)
Frederic Raphael, American-British writer (1931–)

•

He is a lover of his country who rebukes and does not excuse
its sins. It is righteousness that exalteth a nation while sin is a
reproach to any people.
["Love of God, Love of Man, Love of Country" speech
in Syracuse, 1847]
Frederick Douglass, American abolitionist and statesman
(1818–1895)

•

It isn't that they can't see the solution. It is that they can't see
the problem.
The Scandal of Father Brown (1935)
GK Chesterton, English writer and critic (1874–1936)

Democracy substitutes election by the incompetent many for appointment by the corrupt few.
Man and Superman (1903)
George Bernard Shaw, Irish playwright (1856–1950)

•

If the French noblesse had been capable of playing cricket with their peasants, their châteaux would never have been burnt.
English Social History (1942)
GM Trevelyan, British historian (1876–1962)

•

I heartily accept the motto, — "That government is best which governs least" ... Carried out, it finally amounts to this, which I also believe, — "That government is best which governs not at all."
Civil Disobedience (1849)
Henry David Thoreau, American essayist (1817–1862)

•

Everybody talks of the constitution, but all sides forget that the constitution is extremely well, and would do very well, if they would but let it alone.
[Letter, 1770]
Horace Walpole, art historian and writer (1717–1797)

•

Society is based on the assumption that everyone is alike and no one is alive.
Hugh Kingsmill, British journalist (1889–1949)

Guidelines for bureaucrats: (1) When in charge, ponder.
The New York Times (1970)
James Boren, American writer (1925–2010)

•

I can't help feeling wary when I hear anything said about the masses. First you take their faces from 'em by calling 'em the masses and then you accuse 'em of not having any faces.
Saturn Over the Water (1961)
JB Priestley, English playwright and critic (1894–1984)

•

Fear is the foundation of most governments.
Thoughts on Government (1776)
John Adams, 2nd president of the US (1735–1826)

•

Law is a bottomless pit.
The History of John Bull (1727)
John Arbuthnot, Scottish physician and satirist (1667–1735)

•

I think it will be a clash between the political will and the administrative won't.
Yes, Prime Minister (1981)
Jonathan Lynn (1943–) and **Antony Jay** (1930–2016),
English writers

Laws are like cobwebs, which may catch small flies
but let wasps and hornets break through.
A Critical Essay upon the Faculties of the Mind (1709)
Jonathan Swift, Irish poet and satirist (1667–1745)

•

In place of the old bourgeois society, with its classes and
class antagonisms, we shall have an association, in which
the free development of each is the condition for the free
development of all.
The Communist Manifesto (1848)
Karl Marx (1818–1883) and **Friedrich Engels** (1820–1895),
German philosophers

•

It is not the consciousness of men that determines their being,
but, on the contrary, their social being that determines their
consciousness.
A Contribution to the Critique of Political Economy (1859)
Karl Marx, German philosopher (1818–1883)

•

To betray, you must first belong.
The Sunday Times (1967)
Kim Philby, British intelligence officer and Soviet spy (1912–1988)

•

In a hierarchy every employee tends to rise to his level
of incompetence.
The Peter Principle (1969)
Laurence J Peter, Canadian educator (1919–1990)

A lawyer with his briefcase can steal more than a hundred men with guns.
The Godfather (1969)
Mario Puzo, American writer (1920–1999)

•

Never believe governments, not any of them, not a word they say; keep an untrusting eye on all they do.
A Stricken Field (1940)
Martha Gellhorn, American journalist (1908–1998)

•

I want to be the white man's brother, not his brother-in-law.
New York Journal-American (1962)
Martin Luther King Jr, American minister and civil rights activist (1929–1968)

•

We must concentrate not merely on the negative expulsion of war but the positive affirmation of peace.
Martin Luther King Jr, American minister and civil rights activist (1929–1968)

•

One has not only a legal, but a moral responsibility to obey just laws. Conversely, one has a moral responsibility to disobey unjust laws.
[Letter from Birmingham Jail, 1963]
Martin Luther King Jr, American minister and civil rights activist (1929–1968)

The general will rules in society as the private will governs each separate individual.
Lettres à ses commettans (1793)
Maximilien Robespierre, French lawyer and revolutionary leader (1758–1794)

•

Thank heavens we do not get all of the government that we are made to pay for.
[Quoted in the House of Lords, 1994]
Milton Friedman, American economist (1912–2006)

•

An aristocracy in a republic is like a chicken whose head has been cut off; it may run about in a lively way, but in fact it is dead.
Noblesse Oblige: An Enquiry Into the Identifiable Characteristics of the English Aristocracy (1956)
Nancy Mitford, English writer (1904–73)

•

A land that does not like doing things by halves.
Dead Souls (1842)
[Of Russia]
Nikolai Gogol, Russian writer (1809–1852)

•

Laws grind the poor, and rich men rule the law.
The Traveller (1764)
Oliver Goldsmith, Irish writer and dramatist (1728–1774)

Whoever speaks of Europe is wrong, [it is] a geographical concept.
[In a marginal note on a letter, 1876]
Otto von Bismarck, German statesman (1815–1898)

•

Nothing, like something, happens anywhere.
I Remember, I Remember (1955)
Philip Larkin, English poet, writer and librarian (1922–1985)

•

Excess generally causes reaction, and produces a change in the opposite direction, whether it be in the seasons, or in individuals, or in governments.
Plato, Greek philosopher (c. 428/427–348/347 BC)

•

I am constantly amazed by man's inhumanity to man.
Primo Levi, Italian writer, chemist and Holocaust survivor (1919–1987)

•

We have Africa in our blood and Africa has our bones. We are all Africans.
A Devil's Chaplain (2003)
Richard Dawkins, English biologist (1941–)

Ring out the want, the care, the sin
The faithless coldness of the times
Ring out, ring out thy mournful rhyme
but ring the fuller minstrel in.
Ring Out, Wild Bells (1850)
Alfred, Lord Tennyson, English poet (1809–1892)

•

Before I built a wall I'd ask to know
What I was walling in or walling out,
And to whom I was like to give offence.
Mending Wall (1914)
Robert Frost, American poet (1874–1963)

•

Democracy is the name we give the people whenever
we need them.
L'habit vert (1913)
Robert de Flers (1872–1927) and **Gaston Arman de Caillavet**
(1869–1915), French playwrights

•

The Common Law of England has been laboriously built about
a mythical figure — the figure of "The Reasonable Man".
Uncommon Law (1935)
AP Herbert, English writer and activist (1890–1971)

It's every man's business to see justice done.
The Memoirs of Sherlock Holmes (1893)
Sir Arthur Conan Doyle, Scottish writer (1859–1930)

•

What two ideas are more inseparable than beer and Britannia?
Sydney Smith, English wit, writer, and cleric (1771–1845)

•

A man who is good enough to shed his blood for his country is
good enough to be given a square deal afterwards. More than
that no man is entitled to, and less than that no man shall have.
[Speech in Illinois, 1903]
Theodore Roosevelt, 26th president of the US (1858–1919)

•

Thus our democracy was, from an early period, the most
aristocratic, and our aristocracy the most democratic in
the world.
Thomas Babington Macaulay, 1st Baron Macaulay,
British historian and politician (1800–1859)

•

If a nation expects to be ignorant and free, in a state of
civilisation, it expects what never was and never will be.
[Letter to Colonel Charles Yancey, 1816]
Thomas Jefferson, 3rd president of the US (1743–1826)

A little rebellion now and then is a good thing.
[Letter to James Madison, 1787]
Thomas Jefferson, 3rd president of the US (1743–1826)

•

We can't all do everything.
Virgil, Roman poet (70–19 BC)

•

It is an inevitable defect, that bureaucrats will care more
for routine than for results.
The English Constitution (1867)
Walter Bagehot, British journalist, businessman and essayist
(1826–1877)

•

All the world over, I will back the masses against the classes.
[Speech in Liverpool, 1886]
WE Gladstone, prime minister of the UK (1809–1898)

•

The object of government in peace and in war is not the glory
of rulers or of races, but the happiness of the common man.
Social Insurance and Allied Services (1942)
William Henry Beveridge, British economist and social reformer
(1879–1963)

There is something behind the throne greater than the King himself.
[In the House of Lords, 1770]
William Pitt, prime minister of the UK (1708–1778)

•

I know, and all the world knows, that revolutions never go backward.
[Speech, 1858]
William Seward, American politician (1801–1872)

•

Those entrusted with arms ... should be persons of some substance and stake in the country.
[Speech, 1807]
William Windham, British statesman and politician (1750–1810)

•

Where mass hunger reigns, we cannot speak of peace.
World Armament and World Hunger (1986)
Willy Brandt, German politician (1913–1992)

•

Here is a law which is above the King and which even he must not break. This reaffirmation of a supreme law and its expression in a general charter is the great work of Magna Carta; and this alone justifies the respect in which men have held it.
A History of the English-Speaking Peoples (1956)
Sir Winston Churchill, prime minister of the UK, historian and Nobel Prize winner (1874–1965)

I come from a people who gave the ten commandments to the world. Time has come to strengthen them by three additional ones, which we ought to adopt and commit ourselves to: thou shalt not be a perpetrator; thou shalt not be a victim; and thou shalt never, but never, be a bystander.

[Speech to the German Bundestag, 1998]

Yehuda Bauer, Israeli historian (1926–)

GRATITUDE AND TRIBUTE

She would rather light a candle than curse the darkness,
and her glow has warmed the world.
[On learning of Eleanor Roosevelt's death, 1962]
Adlai Stevenson, American politician (1900–1965)

•

Each man in his way is a treasure.
[About the members of his 1910–1913 expedition to Antarctica]
Captain Robert Falcon Scott, British explorer (1868–1912)

•

We often take for granted the very things that most deserve
our gratitude.
Cynthia Ozick, American short-story writer (1928–)

•

When you go home, tell them of us and say, "For your tomorrows
these gave their today."
John Maxwell Edmonds, English classicist (1875–1958)

•

Every time I create an appointment, I create a hundred
malcontents and one ingrate.
Louis XIV, King of France (1638–1715)

•

If you see no reason for giving thanks, the fault lies in yourself
Native American proverb (Minquass)

Here lies one who meant well, tried a little, failed much: —
surely that may be his epitaph, of which he need not
be ashamed.
Across the Plains (1892)
Robert Louis Stevenson, Scottish writer (1850–1894)

•

Only when you have eaten a lemon do you appreciate what
sugar is.
Ukrainian proverb

•

Most human beings have an almost infinite capacity for taking
things for granted.
Themes and Variations (1950)
Aldous Huxley, English writer and philosopher (1894–1963)

•

There are no limits to human ingratitude.
No One Writes to the Colonel (1961)
Gabriel García Márquez, Colombian writer (1927–2014)

•

In Hollywood gratitude is Public Enemy Number One.
From Under My Hat (1952)
Hedda Hopper, American actress and gossip columnist
(1885–1966)

Over-great haste to repay an obligation is a form of ingratitude.
Maximes (1678)
François de La Rochefoucauld, French writer (1613–1680)

•

I once knew a man out of courtesy help a lame dog over a stile,
and he for requital bit his fingers.
The Religion of Protestants (1637)
William Chillingworth, English churchman (1602–1644)

•

Blow, blow, thou winter wind,
Thou art not so unkind
As man's ingratitude; …
Freeze, freeze, thou bitter sky,
That dost not bite so nigh
As benefits forgot.
As You Like It (1603)
William Shakespeare, English poet and dramatist (1564–1616)

•

Hereabouts died a very gallant gentleman, Captain LEG Oates
of the Inniskilling Dragoons. In March 1912, returning from the
Pole, he walked willingly to his death in a blizzard, to try and
save his comrades, beset by hardships.
[Epitaph on a cairn and cross erected in the Antarctic, 1912]
Surgeon-Captain EL Atkinson, Royal Navy surgeon (1881–1929)

HAPPINESS AND TORMENT

Happiness is not a goal … it's a by-product of a life well lived.
Eleanor Roosevelt, first lady of the US (1884–1962)

•

Every day, in every way, I am getting better and better.
Émile Coué, French psychologist (1857–1926)

•

That action is best, which procures the greatest happiness
for the greatest numbers.
Francis Hutcheson, Irish philosopher (1694–1746)

•

Human happiness and moral duty are inseparably connected.
George Washington, 1st president of the US (1732–1799)

•

Now and then it's good to pause in our pursuit of happiness
and just be happy.
Guillaume Apollinaire, French poet (1880–1918)

•

Success is not the key to happiness. Happiness is the
key to success.
Omaha World Herald (1996)
Herman Cain, American businessman (1945–)

The most hateful torment for men is to have knowledge
of everything but power over nothing.
Herodotus, Greek historian (485–425 BC)

•

The whole secret of life is to be interested in one thing
profoundly and in a thousand things well.
Horace Walpole, English art historian and writer (1717–1797)

•

A contented mind is the greatest blessing a man can enjoy
in this world.
Joseph Addison, English essayist (1672–1719)

•

If you want to be happy, be.
Leo Tolstoy, Russian writer (1828–1910)

•

Live, and be happy, and make others so.
Frankenstein (1823)
Mary Shelley, English writer (1797–1851)

•

And Charlie, don't forget about what happened to the man
who suddenly got everything he ever wanted. He lived happily
ever after.
Charlie and the Chocolate Factory (1964)
Roald Dahl, British writer (1916–1990)

Happiness makes up in height for what it lacks in length.
Robert Frost, American poet (1874–1963)

•

Pleasure is very seldom found where it is sought. Our brightest
blazes are commonly kindled by unexpected sparks.
Samuel Johnson, English writer, critic and lexicographer
(1709–1784)

•

Hope is the cordial that keeps life from stagnating.
Samuel Richardson, English writer (1689–1761)

•

How happy is he born and taught
That serveth not another's will;
Whose armour is his honest thought,
And simple truth his utmost skill!
Sir Henry Wotton, English poet and diplomat (1568–1639)

•

Nobody owns anything but everyone is rich — for what greater
wealth can there be than cheerfulness, peace of mind, and
freedom from anxiety?
Utopia (1516)
Sir Thomas More, English saint and lawyer (1478–1535)

•

The supreme happiness in life is the conviction that we are loved.
Victor Hugo, French poet, writer, and dramatist (1802–1885)

It is not true that suffering ennobles the character; happiness does that sometimes, but suffering, for the most part, makes men petty and vindictive.
The Moon and Sixpence (1919)
W Somerset Maugham, British writer and playwright
(1874–1965)

•

To fill the hour — that is happiness.
Essays, Second Series (1844)
Ralph Waldo Emerson, American poet, essayist and philosopher
(1803–1882)

•

In Hollywood, if you don't have happiness, you send out for it.
Colombo's Hollywood (1979)
Rex Reed, American film critic (1938–)

•

Happiness is no laughing matter.
Apophthegms (1854)
Richard Whately, English economist (1787–1863)

HEALTH AND WELLBEING

Every man is the builder of a temple, called his body.
Walden (1854)
Henry David Thoreau, American writer and philosopher
(1817–1862)

.

Everyone wants to live long but no one wants to be called old.
Icelandic proverb

.

We are healed of a suffering only by experiencing it to the full.
Albertine disparue (1927)
Marcel Proust, French writer (1871–1922)

.

Oh Sleep! it is a gentle thing,
Beloved from pole to pole.
The Rime of the Ancient Mariner (1798)
Samuel Taylor Coleridge, English poet (1772-1834)

.

The sovereign invigorator of the body is exercise, and of all
the exercises, walking is best.
Thomas Jefferson, 3rd president of the US (1743–1826)

Most of the time we think we're sick, it's all in the mind.
Look Homeward, Angel (1929)
Thomas Wolfe, American writer (1900–1938)

•

One cannot think well, love well, sleep well, if one has not dined well.
A Room of One's Own (1929)
Virginia Woolf, English writer (1882–1941)

•

Sleep is when all the unsorted stuff comes flying out as from a dustbin upset in a high wind.
Pincher Martin (1956)
William Golding, British writer (1911–1993)

•

Not to be healthy ... is one of the few sins that modern society is willing to recognise and condemn.
The Cunning Man (1994)
Robertson Davies, Canadian writer (1913–1995)

•

I am convinced digestion is the great secret of life.
[Letter to Arthur Kinglake, 1837]
Sydney Smith, English wit, writer and cleric (1771–1845)

•

Make hunger thy sauce, as a medicine for health.
Five Hundred Points of Good Husbandry (1557)
Thomas Tusser, English poet (1524–1580)

Thousands upon thousands of persons have studied disease.
Almost no one has studied health.
Let's Eat Right to Keep Fit (1954)
Adelle Davis, American writer (1904–1974)

•

Exercise is bunk. If you are healthy, you don't need it:
if you are sick you shouldn't take it.
[Attr.]
Henry Ford, American industrialist and businessman
(1863–1947)

•

Happiness is good health — and a bad memory.
Ingrid Bergman, Swedish actress (1915–1982)

•

Look to your health; and if you have it, praise God, and value it
next to a good conscience; for health is the second blessing that
we mortals are capable of; a blessing money cannot buy.
The Compleat Angler (1653)
Izaak Walton, English writer (1593–1683)

•

Early to rise and early to bed makes a male healthy and wealthy
and dead.
The New Yorker (1939)
James Thurber, American cartoonist (1894–1961)

HISTORY AND THE PAST

History teaches us that men and nations behave wisely once
they have exhausted all other alternatives.
[Speech, 1970]
Abba Eban, Israeli diplomat, politician and scholar (1915–2002)

•

Memory says: Want to do right? Don't count on me.
Eastern War Time (1991)
Adrienne Rich, American poet and critic (1929–2012)

•

Human blunders, usually, do more to shape history than
human wickedness.
The Origins of the Second World War (1961)
AJP Taylor, English historian (1906–1990)

•

That men do not learn very much from the lessons of history is
the most important of all the lessons that history has to teach.
Collected Essays (1959)
Aldous Huxley, English writer and philosopher (1894–1963)

•

History is a gallery of pictures in which there are few originals
and many copies.
L'Ancien Régime et la Révolution (1856)
Alexis de Tocqueville, French diplomat and political theorist
(1805–1859)

If you want the present to be different from the past, study the past.
Baruch Spinoza, Dutch philosopher (1632–1677)

•

Better by far you should forget and smile
Than that you should remember and be sad.
Remember (1862)
Christina Rossetti, English poet (1830–1894)

•

Unless we remember we cannot understand.
Aspects of the Novel (1927)
EM Forster, English writer (1879–1970)

•

There is no present or future, only the past, happening over and over again, now.
A Moon for the Misbegotten (1947)
Eugene O'Neill, American playwright (1888–1953)

•

Those who cannot remember the past are condemned to repeat it.
The Life of Reason (1906)
George Santayana, Spanish philosopher and writer (1863–1952)

What experience and history teach is this — that nations
and governments have never learned anything from history,
or acted upon any lessons they might have drawn from it.
Lectures on the Philosophy of History (1830)
GWF Hegel, German philosopher (1770–1831)

•

The supreme purpose of history is a better world.
Herbert Hoover, 31st president of the US (1874–1964)

•

History is a combination of reality and lies. The reality of history
becomes a lie. The unreality of the fable becomes the truth.
Journal d'un inconnu (1953)
Jean Cocteau, French writer and dramatist (1889–1963)

•

They spend their time mostly looking forward to the past.
Look Back in Anger (1956)
John Osborne, English playwright, actor and screenwriter
(1929–1994)

•

Our duty is to preserve what the past has had to say for itself,
and to say for ourselves what shall be true for the future.
[Attr.]
John Ruskin, English art critic (1819–1900)

Ignorance is the first requisite of the historian — ignorance, which simplifies and clarifies, which selects and omits, with a placid perfection unattainable by the highest art.
Eminent Victorians (1918)
Lytton Strachey, English writer and critic (1880–1932)

•

History is the version of past events that people have decided to agree upon.
Napoleon Bonaparte, French statesman and military leader (1769–1821)

•

Memory... is the diary we all carry about with us.
The Importance of Being Earnest (1895)
Oscar Wilde, Irish dramatist and poet (1854–1900)

•

The one duty we owe to history is to rewrite it.
Intentions (1891)
Oscar Wilde, Irish dramatist and poet (1854–1900)

•

History is a cyclic poem written by time upon the memories of man.
A Defence of Poetry (1821)
Percy Bysshe Shelley, English poet (1792–1822)

If history were taught in the form of stories, it would never be forgotten.
Rudyard Kipling, English journalist and writer (1865–1936)

•

George the First knew nothing, and desired to know nothing; did nothing, and desired to do nothing; and the only good thing that is told of him is, that he wished to restore the crown to its hereditary successor.
Samuel Johnson, English writer, critic and lexicographer (1709–1784)

•

Not the power to remember, but its very opposite, the power to forget, is a necessary condition for our existence.
The Nazarene (1939)
Sholem Asch, Polish-Jewish writer and dramatist (1880–1957)

•

There is no history of mankind, there are only many histories of all kinds of aspects of human life. And one of these is the history of political power. This is elevated into the history of the world.
The Open Society and its Enemies (1945)
Sir Karl Popper, Austrian-British philosopher and professor (1902–1994)

•

[History] hath triumphed over time, which besides it, nothing but eternity hath triumphed over.
The History of the World (1614)
Sir Walter Raleigh, English writer and statesman (1552–1618)

For last year's words belong to last year's language
And next year's words await another voice.
Four Quartets (1943)
TS Eliot, English-American poet, critic and dramatist (1888–1965)

•

They plucked communion-tables down
And broke our painted glasses
They threw our altars to the ground
And tumbled down the crosses
They set up Cromwell and his heir
The Lord and Lady Claypole
Because they hated Common Prayer
The organ and the maypole.
How the War Began (1664)
Thomas Jordan, English poet, actor and playwright (1612–1685)

•

When to the sessions of sweet silent thought
I summon up remembrance of things past,
I sigh the lack of many a thing I sought,
And with old woes new wail my dear time's waste.
Sonnet 30 (1609)
William Shakespeare, English poet and dramatist (1564–1616)

•

It is like writing history with lightning. And my only regret
is that it is all so terribly true.
[On seeing the Civil War film *The Birth of a Nation* at the
White House in 1915]
Woodrow Wilson, 28th president of the US (1856–1924)

HOPE

Hope is itself a species of happiness, and, perhaps, the chief happiness which this world affords.
Samuel Johnson, English writer, critic and lexicographer (1709–1784)

•

What man is strong enough to reject the possibility of hope?
The Locked Room (1986)
Paul Auster, American writer (1947–)

•

Even if the hopes you started out with are dashed,
hope has to be maintained.
Seamus Heaney, Irish poet, playwright and translator (1939–2013)

•

Hope springs eternal in the human breast;
Man never is, but always to be blest.
An Essay on Man (1733)
Alexander Pope, English poet (1688–1744)

INTELLIGENCE AND IDEAS

The height of cleverness is to be able to conceal it.
Maximes (1678)
François de La Rochefoucauld, French writer (1613–1680)

•

The intelligent are to the intelligentsia what a gentleman
is to a gent.
Stanley Baldwin, prime minister of the UK (1867–1947)

•

What is a highbrow? He is a man who has found something
more interesting than women.
New York Times (1932)
Edgar Wallace, English writer (1875–1932)

•

I am patient with stupidity but not with those who are
proud of it.
Edith Sitwell, British poet and critic (1887–1964)

•

Little minds are interested in the extraordinary;
great minds in the commonplace.
A Thousand and One Epigrams (1911)
Elbert Hubbard, American writer (1856–1915)

It takes something more than intelligence to act intelligently.
Crime and Punishment (1866)
Fyodor Dostoyevsky, Russian writer (1821–1881)

•

Think like a man of action, act like a man of thought.
Henri Bergson, French philosopher (1859–1941)

•

The surface of the earth is soft and impressible by the feet
of men; and so with the paths which the mind travels.
Walden (1854)
Henry David Thoreau, American writer and philosopher
(1817–1862)

•

As soon as an idea is accepted it is time to reject it.
Platitudes in the Making (1911)
Holbrook Jackson, English writer and critic (1874–1948)

•

Dare to know! Have the courage to use your own reason!
This is the motto of the Enlightenment.
What is Enlightenment? (1784)
Immanuel Kant, German philosopher (1724–1804)

•

My mind is not a bed to be made and remade.
Ego 6 (1944)
James Agate, English drama critic and writer (1877–1947)

The English approach to ideas is not to kill them,
but to let them die slowly of neglect.
The English: A Portrait of a People (1998)
Jeremy Paxman, British broadcaster (1950–)

•

The only means of strengthening one's intellect is to make up
one's mind about nothing — to let the mind be a thoroughfare
for all thoughts. Not a select party.
John Keats, English poet (1795–1821)

•

New opinions are always suspected, and usually opposed,
without any other reason but because they are not already
common.
An Essay Concerning Human Understanding (1690)
John Locke, English philosopher (1632–1704)

•

Ideas shape the course of history.
John Maynard Keynes, British economist (1883–1946)

•

Handle a book as a bee does a flower, extract its sweetness
but do not damage it.
John Muir, Scottish-American naturalist and writer
(1838–1914)

The brightest flashes in the world of thought are incomplete until they have been proved to have their counterparts in the world of fact.
Fragments of Science, Vol II (1879)
John Tyndall, Irish physicist (1820–1893)

•

There's nothing of so infinite vexation as man's own thoughts.
The White Devil (1612)
John Webster, English dramatist (c. 1580–1634)

•

Respond intelligently even to unintelligent treatment.
Tao Te Ching
Lao Tzu, Chinese philosopher (?-533 BC)

•

The philosopher's treatment of a question is like the treatment of an illness.
Philosophical Investigations (1953)
Ludwig Wittgenstein, Austrian-born philosopher (1889–1951)

•

I must have a prodigious quantity of mind; it takes me as much as a week, sometimes, to make it up.
The Innocents Abroad (1869)
Mark Twain, American writer (1835–1910)

Mystery creates wonder and wonder is the basis of man's desire to understand.
Neil Armstrong, American astronaut (1930–2012)

•

It is better to entertain an idea than to take it home to live with you for the rest of your life.
Pictures from an Institution (1954)
Randall Jarrell, American poet (1914–1965)

•

We can lift ourselves out of ignorance, we can find ourselves as creatures of excellence and intelligence and skill.
Jonathan Livingston Seagull (1970)
Richard Bach, American writer (1936–)

•

That's the classical mind at work, runs fine inside but looks dingy on the surface.
Zen and the Art of Motorcycle Maintenance
Robert M Pirsig, American writer (1928–2017)

•

The true genius is a mind of large general powers, accidentally determined to some particular direction.
Lives of the English Poets (1779–81)
Samuel Johnson, English writer, critic and lexicographer (1709–1784)

Of all the ruins that of a noble mind is the most deplorable.
The Adventure of the Dying Detective (1913)
Sir Arthur Conan Doyle, Scottish writer (1859–1930)

•

Men are never so good or so bad as their opinions.
Sir James Mackintosh, Scottish politician (1765–1832)

•

I have striven not to laugh at human actions, not to weep
at them, not to hate them, but to understand them.
Baruch Spinoza, Dutch philosopher (1632–1677)

•

A man does not attain the status of Galileo merely because
he is persecuted; he must also be right.
Ever Since Darwin (1977)
Stephen Jay Gould, American palaeontologist (1941–2002)

•

Is there no way out of the mind?
Apprehensions (1971)
Sylvia Plath, American poet and writer (1932–1963)

•

The end of man is an action and not a thought,
though it were the noblest.
Sartor Resartus (1834)
Thomas Carlyle, Scottish philosopher and historian (1795–1881)

Action is the proper fruit of knowledge.
Thomas Fuller, English churchman and historian (1608–1661)

•

If one does not reflect, one thinks oneself master of everything;
but when one does reflect, one realises that one is master of
nothing.
Voltaire, French writer and philosopher (1694–1778)

•

The palm at the end of the mind,
Beyond the last thought, rises.
Of Mere Being (1957)
Wallace Stevens, American poet (1879–1955)

•

Do I contradict myself?
Very well then I contradict myself,
(I am large, I contain multitudes.)
Song of Myself (1855)
Walt Whitman, American poet (1819–1892)

•

He, who will not reason, is a bigot; he, who cannot, is a fool;
and he, who dares not, is a slave.
Heretics are the only bitter remedy against the entropy of
human thought.
Academical Questions (1805)
William Drummond of Logiealmond, Scottish diplomat
and philosopher (1770–1828)

Every intellectual attitude is latently political.
Thomas Mann, German writer and social critic (1875–1955)

•

Brevity is the soul of wit.
Hamlet, Act II (c. 1600)
William Shakespeare, English poet and dramatist (1564–1616)

•

My brain: it's my second favourite organ.
Sleeper (1973)
Woody Allen, American film director and actor (1935–)

•

A good newspaper, I suppose, is a nation talking to itself.
The Observer (1961)
Arthur Miller, American playwright (1915–2005)

•

It is a good thing for an uneducated man to read books
of quotations.
Sir Winston Churchill, prime minister of the UK, historian and
Nobel Prize winner (1874–1965)

JUDGMENT AND WORTH

It is easier to know man in general than to know one man in particular.
Maximes (1665)
François de La Rochefoucauld, French writer (1613–1680)

.

The glory of great men should always be measured against the means they used to acquire it.
Maximes (1665)
François de La Rochefoucauld, French writer (1613–1680)

.

How easy it is to judge rightly after one sees what evil comes from judging wrongly.
Wives and Daughters (1864)
Elizabeth Gaskell, English writer (1810–1865)

.

Don't judge a man by his opinions, but what his opinions have made of him.
Georg Christoph Lichtenberg, German physicist and satirist (1742–1799)

To judge a thing that has substance and solid worth is quite easy, to comprehend it is much harder, and to blend judgment and comprehension in a definitive description is the hardest thing of all.

The Phenomenology of Spirit (1807)

GWF Hegel, German philosopher
(1770–1831)

•

Out of the crooked timber of humanity no straight thing can ever be made.

Idea for a Universal History with a Cosmopolitan Purpose (1784)

Immanuel Kant, German philosopher (1724–1804)

•

It is often said that second thoughts are best. So they are in matters of judgment but not in matters of conscience.

John Henry Newman, English poet and cardinal
(1801–1890)

•

It is better for a leader to make a mistake in forgiving than to make a mistake in punishing.

Prophet Muhammad (571–632)

•

The worth of a soul cannot be told.

Unknown, possibly **Olaudah Equiano (Gustavus Vassa)**, writer and abolitionist (1745–1797)

I would rather have a plain russet-coated captain that knows
what he fights for, and loves what he knows, than that which
you call "a gentleman" and is nothing else.
[Letter to Sir William Spring, 1643]
Oliver Cromwell, English military and political leader
(1599–1658)

•

His doubts are better than most people's certainties.
Philip Yorke, 1st Earl of Hardwicke, English lawyer
and politician (1690–1764)

•

A judge must bear in mind that when he tries a case he is
himself on trial.
Special Laws (1st century)
Philo, Hellenized Jewish philosopher (25 BC–AD 50)

•

It is a capital mistake to theorise before one has data.
It biases the judgment.
A Study in Scarlet (1887)
Sir Arthur Conan Doyle, Scottish writer (1859–1930)

•

The being without an opinion is so painful to human nature that
most people will leap to a hasty opinion rather than undergo it.
The Economist (c. 1875)
Walter Bagehot, British journalist, businessman and essayist
(1826–1877)

Appearances are not held to be a clue to the truth.

But we seem to have no other.

Manservant and Maidservant (1947)

Ivy Compton-Burnett, English writer (1884–1969)

LEADERSHIP

Setting an example is not the main means of influencing others, it is the only means.
Albert Einstein, German theoretical physicist (1879–1955)

.

The led must not be compelled, they must be able to choose their own leader.
Albert Einstein, German theoretical physicist (1879–1955)

.

An army of sheep led by a lion would defeat an army of lions led by a sheep.
Arab proverb or **Alexander the Great**, King of Macedon (356–323 BC)

.

The trouble in modern democracy is that men do not approach to leadership until they have lost the desire to lead anyone.
The Observer
William Henry Beveridge, British economist and social reformer (1879–1963)

.

The high sentiments always win in the end, leaders who offer blood, toil, tears and sweat always get more out of their followers than those who offer safety and a good time. When it comes to the pinch, human beings are heroic.
Horizon (1941)
George Orwell, English writer (1903–1950)

LIFE, OR THE WAY OF THE WORLD

Man is born unto trouble, as the sparks fly upward.
The Bible
Job 5:7

•

Life is a tragedy when seen in close-up, but a comedy in long-shot.
Charlie Chaplin, English comic actor, director and composer (1889–1977)

•

Life is a foreign language: all men mispronounce it.
Thunder on the Left (1925)
Christopher Morley, American writer (1890–1957)

•

Only the flow matters: live and let live, love and let love. There is no point to love and life.
Do Women Change? (1930)
DH Lawrence, English writer and poet (1885–1930)

•

One is never as unhappy as one thinks, nor as happy as one hopes.
Sentences et Maximes de Morale (1664)
François de La Rochefoucauld, French writer (1613–1680)

Oh, isn't life a terrible thing, thank God?
Under Milk Wood (1954)
Dylan Thomas, Welsh writer (1914–1953)

·

If you look at life one way, there is always cause for alarm.
The Death of the Heart (1938)
Elizabeth Bowen, Irish writer (1899–1973)

·

I slept, and dreamed that life was beauty; I woke, and found that
life was duty.
Beauty and Duty (1840)
Ellen Sturgis Hooper, American poet (1812–1848)

·

The world is the best of all possible worlds, and everything
in it is a necessary evil.
Appearance and Reality (1893)
FH Bradley, British philosopher (1846–1924)

·

Life is something to do when you can't get to sleep.
Metropolitan Life (1978)
Fran Lebowitz, American writer and public speaker (1950–)

·

Everybody gets so much information all day long that they lose
their common sense.
Reflection on the Atomic Bomb (1946)
Gertrude Stein, American writer (1874–1946)

Finality is death. Perfection is finality. Nothing is perfect.
There are lumps in it.
The Crock of Gold (1912)
James Stephens, Irish writer (1880–1950)

•

For what do we live, but to make sport for our neighbours,
and laugh at them in our turn?
Pride and Prejudice (1813)
Jane Austen, English writer (1775–1817)

•

We can't all be happy, we can't all be rich, we can't all be lucky …
Some must cry so that others may be able to laugh the
more heartily.
Good Morning, Midnight (1939)
Jean Rhys, Dominican writer (1890–1979)

•

We are merely the stars' tennis balls, struck and bandied
Which way please them.
The Duchess of Malfi (1614)
John Webster, English dramatist (c. 1580–1634)

•

Books say: she did this because. Life says: she did this.
Books are where things are explained to you; life is where
things aren't.
Flaubert's Parrot (1984)
Julian Barnes, English writer (1946–)

You get tragedy where the tree, instead of bending, breaks.
Culture and Value (1929)
Ludwig Wittgenstein, Austrian-born philosopher (1889–1951)

•

Death and taxes and childbirth! There's never any convenient
time for any of them.
Gone with the Wind (1936)
Margaret Mitchell, American writer (1900–1949)

•

Ill news hath wings, and with the wind doth go,
Comfort's a cripple and comes ever slow.
The Barons' Wars (1603)
Michael Drayton, English poet (1563–1631)

•

I do not believe that friends are necessarily the people
you like best, they are merely the people who got there first.
Dear Me (1977)
Peter Ustinov, English actor, director and writer
(1921–2004)

•

Life is first boredom, then fear.
Dockery and Son (1964)
Philip Larkin, English poet, writer and librarian (1922–1985)

The cry of the Little Peoples goes up to God in vain,
For the world is given over to the cruel sons of Cain.
The Cry of the Little Peoples (1899)
Richard Le Gallienne, English poet (1866–1947)

•

It is a folly to expect men to do all that they may reasonably be
expected to do.
Apophthegms (1854)
Richard Whately, English philosopher and theologian (1787–1863)

•

Life is too much like a pathless wood where your face burns and
tickles with the cobwebs broken across it, and one eye is weeping
from a twig's having lashed across it open.
Birches (1916)
Robert Frost, American poet (1874–1963)

•

Life is not a matter of holding good cards, but of playing
a poor hand well.
Robert Louis Stevenson, Scottish writer (1850–1894)

•

You will put on a dress of guilt and shoes with broken
high ideals.
Comeclose and Sleepnow (1967)
Roger McGough, English writer, dramatist and broadcaster
(1937–)

The world is disgracefully managed, one hardly knows
to whom to complain.
Vainglory (1915)
Ronald Firbank, English writer (1886–1926)

•

Most of what matters in your life takes place in your absence.
Midnight's Children (1981)
Salman Rushdie, British-Indian writer (1947–)

•

Life is like playing a violin solo in public and learning the
instrument as one goes on.
[Speech at the Somerville Club, 1895]
Samuel Butler, English writer (1835–1902)

•

To live is like to love — all reason is against it, and all healthy
instinct for it.
Notebooks (1912)
Samuel Butler, English writer (1835–1902)

•

We would all be idle if we could.
Samuel Johnson, English writer, critic and lexicographer
(1709–1784)

Life can only be understood backwards, but it must be lived forwards.
The Journals of Søren Kierkegaard (1938)
Søren Kierkegaard, Danish philosopher (1813–1855)

•

Life is an unanswered question, but let's still believe in the dignity and importance of the question.
The New York Times (1960)
Tennessee Williams, American playwright (1911–1983)

•

At high tide the fish eat ants; at low tide the ants eat fish.
Thai proverb

•

This hobble of being alive is rather serious, don't you think so?
Tess of the d'Urbervilles (1891)
Thomas Hardy, English writer and poet (1840–1928)

•

I have lost friends, some by death ... others through sheer inability to cross the street.
The Waves (1931)
Virginia Woolf, English writer (1882–1941)

•

It is a very funny thing about life; if you refuse to accept anything but the best, you very often get it.
W Somerset Maugham, British playwright (1874–1965)

Life is not a set campaign, but an irregular work, and the main forces in it are not overt resolutions, but latent and half-involuntary promptings.
Walter Bagehot, British journalist, businessman and essayist (1826–1877)

•

I know that's a secret, for it's whispered everywhere.
Love for Love (1695)
William Congreve, English dramatist and poet (1670–1729)

•

Variety's the very spice of life, that gives it all its flavour.
The Task (1785)
William Cowper, English poet and hymnodist (1731–1800)

•

If the world were good for nothing else, it is a fine subject for speculation.
Characteristics: In the Manner of Rochefoucauld's Maxims (1823)
William Hazlitt, English writer and critic (1778–1830)

LOVE AND MARRIAGE

We always deceive ourselves twice about the people we love —
first to their advantage, then to their disadvantage.
A Happy Death (1971)
Albert Camus, French philosopher, writer and journalist
(1913–1960)

•

The fate of love is that it always seems too little or
too much.
The Belle of Bowling Green (1904)
Amelia Edith Barr, British-American writer (1831–1919)

•

Life has taught us that love does not consist in gazing at each
other but in looking together in the same direction.
Terre des Hommes (1939)
Antoine de Saint-Exupéry, French writer (1900–1944)

•

To fear love is to fear life, and those who fear life are already
three parts dead.
Marriage and Morals (1929)
Bertrand Russell, British philosopher, mathematician,
historian and writer (1872–1970)

Of all forms of caution, caution in love is perhaps the most fatal to true happiness.
The Conquest of Happiness (1930)
Bertrand Russell, British philosopher, mathematician, historian and writer (1872–1970)

•

Most people experience love, without noticing that there is anything remarkable about it.
Doctor Zhivago (1957)
Boris Pasternak, Russian writer and literary translator (1890–1960)

•

How selfhood begins with a walking away, and love is proved in the letting go.
Walking Away (1956)
Cecil Day-Lewis, Anglo-Irish poet (1904–1972)

•

Love's like the measles — all the worse when it comes late in life.
The Wit and Opinions of Douglas Jerrold (1858)
Douglas Jerrold, English playwright and journalist (1803–1857)

•

A crowd is not company, and faces are but a gallery of pictures, and talk but a tinkling cymbal, where there is no love.
Essays (1597)
Francis Bacon, English philosopher, statesman and essayist (1561–1626)

The trouble with marriage is that it ends every night after making love, and it must be rebuilt every morning before breakfast.
Love in the Time of Cholera (1985)
Gabriel García Márquez, Colombian writer (1927–2014)

•

Continental people have sex lives; the English have hot-water bottles.
How to be an Alien (1946)
George Mikes, Hungarian-born British humourist and writer (1912–1987)

•

Love and scandal are the best sweeteners of tea.
Love in Several Masques (1728)
Henry Fielding, English writer and dramatist (1707–1754)

•

Love is the delusion that one woman differs from another.
A Mencken Chrestomathy (1949)
HL Mencken, American journalist and satirist (1880–1956)

•

Free me, I pray, to go in search of Joys Unembroidered by your high, soft voice Along that stony path the senses pave.
The Changing Light at Sandover (1982)
James Merrill, American poet (1926–1995)

You know very well that love is, above all, the gift of oneself!
Ardèle ou la Marguerite (1948)
Jean Anouilh, French dramatist (1910–1987)

•

You should have a softer pillow than my heart.
[Letter to his wife]
George Gordon, Lord Byron, English nobleman and poet (1788–1824)

•

Love is not breathlessness, it is not excitement, it is not the
promulgation of promises of eternal passion. That is just being
"in love" which any of us can convince ourselves we are. Love
itself is what is left over when being in love has burned away,
and this is both an art and a fortunate accident.
Captain Corelli's Mandolin (1994)
Louis de Bernières, British writer (1954–)

•

To me it seems that it is madder never to abandon oneself,
than often to be infatuated; better to be wounded, a captive,
and a slave, than always to walk in armour.
Summer on the Lakes, in 1843 (1844)
Margaret Fuller, American journalist and critic (1810–1850)

•

Maybe the most that you can expect from a relationship
that goes bad is to come out of it with a few good songs.
Faithfull: An Autobiography (1994)
Marianne Faithfull, English singer, songwriter and actress
(1946–)

There is nothing safe about sex. There never will be.
The International Herald Tribune (1992)
Norman Mailer, American writer (1923–2007)

•

Love is free; it is not practised as a way of achieving other ends.
Deus Caritas Est (2005)
Pope Benedict XVI (1927–)

•

The formula for achieving a successful relationship:
You should treat all disasters as if they were trivialities
but never treat a triviality as if it were a disaster.
Manners from Heaven (1984)
Quentin Crisp, English writer, raconteur and actor (1908–1999)

•

I hold this to be the highest task of a bond between two people:
that each should stand guard over the solitude of the other.
Gesammelte Briefe in sechs Bänden (1936)
Rainer Maria Rilke, Austrian poet and writer (1875–1926)

•

Is not marriage an open question, when it is alleged, from
the beginning of the world, that such who are in the institution
wish to get out; and such as are out wish to get in.
Representative Men (1850)
Ralph Waldo Emerson, American poet, essayist and philosopher
(1803–1882)

When one has once fully entered the realm of love, the world —
no matter how imperfect — becomes rich and beautiful, it
consists solely of opportunities for love.
Works of Love (1847)
Søren Kierkegaard, Danish philosopher (1813–1855)

•

The things that we love tell us what we are.
Saint Thomas Aquinas, Italian Catholic priest (1225–1274)

•

By God, DH Lawrence was right when he had said there must
be a dumb, dark dull, bitter belly-tension between a man and a
woman, and how else could this be achieved save in the long
monotony of marriage?
Cold Comfort Farm (1932)
Stella Gibbons, English writer (1902–1989)

•

If you cannot have your dear husband for a comfort and a
delight, for a breadwinner and a crosspatch, for a sofa, chair,
or a hot-water bottle, one can use him as a cross to be borne.
Novel on Yellow Paper (1936)
Stevie Smith, English poet and writer (1902–1971)

•

Marriage, to women as to men, must be a luxury, not a necessity;
an incident of life, not all of it.
Susan B Anthony, American social reformer and women's rights
activist (1820–1906)

My definition of marriage ... it resembles a pair of shears,
so joined that they cannot be separated; often moving in
opposite directions, yet always punishing anyone who comes
between them.
[In *A Memoir of the Reverend Sydney Smith* (1855) by his daughter,
Lady Holland]
Sydney Smith, English wit, writer and cleric (1771–1845)

•

Don't cry because it's over. Smile because it happened.
Theodor Seuss Geisel (Dr Seuss), American writer and cartoonist
(1904–1991)

•

If love is the best thing in life, then the best part of love
is the kiss.
Lotte in Weimar: The Beloved Returns (1939)
Thomas Mann, German writer and social critic (1875–1955)

•

Courtship to marriage, as a very witty prologue to a very
dull play.
The Old Bachelor (1693)
William Congreve, English dramatist and poet (1670–1729)

•

Love? What is it? Most natural painkiller. What there is ... LOVE.
Last Words: The Final Journals (1993)
William S Burroughs, American writer and visual artist
(1914–1997)

And yet, by heaven, I think my love as rare
As any she belied with false compare.
Sonnet 130 (1609)
William Shakespeare, English poet and dramatist (1564–1616)

•

A man in love is incomplete until he has married.
Then he's finished.
Newsweek (1960)
Zsa Zsa Gabor, Hungarian-American actress and socialite
(1917–2016)

•

Husbands are like fires. They go out when unattended.
Newsweek (1960)
Zsa Zsa Gabor, Hungarian-American actress and socialite
(1917–2016)

•

I never hated a man enough to give him his diamonds back.
The Observer (1957)
Zsa Zsa Gabor, Hungarian-American actress and socialite
(1917–2016)

•

Tomorrow our marriage will be 21 years old! How many a storm
has swept over it and still it continues green and fresh and
throws out vigorous roots.
Albert, Prince Consort, husband and consort of Queen Victoria
(1819–1861)

"What is the difference between marriage and prison?"
"In prison somebody else does the cooking."
Andrea Newman, English writer (1938–)

•

Being a husband is a whole-time job. That is why so many
husbands fail. They cannot give their entire attention to it.
The Title: A Comedy in Three Acts (1918)
Arnold Bennett, English writer (1867–1931)

•

He that loves not his wife and children, feeds a lioness at home
and broods a nest of sorrows.
XXV Sermons Preached at Golden Grove (1653)
Jeremy Taylor, English cleric (1613–1667)

•

… the great wonderful construct which is marriage – a construct
made up of a hundred little kindnesses, a thousand little bitings
back of spite, tens of thousands of minor actions of good intent
– this must not, as an institution, be brought down in ruins.
Splitting (1995)
Fay Weldon, English feminist and playwright (1931–)

•

He that hath wife and children, hath given hostages to fortune;
for they are impediments to great enterprises, either of virtue
or mischief.
Francis Bacon, English philosopher, statesman and essayist
(1561–1626)

The roaring of the wind is my wife and the stars through the window pane are my children.
[Letter, 1818]
John Keats, English poet (1795–1821)

MANKIND AND CIVILISATION

Humanity will ever seek but never attain perfection.
Let us at least survive and go on trying.
The Religion of the Machine Age (1983)
Dora Russell, English writer and social activist (1894–1986)

•

Humanity I love you because when you're hard up you pawn
your intelligence to buy a drink.
EE Cummings, American poet (1894–1962)

•

If [human life] depends on anything, it is on this frail cord, flung
from the forgotten hills of yesterday to the invisible mountains
of tomorrow.
The Appetite of Tyranny (1915)
GK Chesterton, English writer (1874–1936)

•

I think there's just one kind of folks. Folks.
To Kill A Mockingbird (1960)
Harper Lee, American writer (1926–2016)

•

All civilisation has from time to time become a thin crust over
a volcano of revolution.
Little Essays of Love and Virtue (1922)
Havelock Ellis, British psychologist (1859–1939)

We cannot live only for ourselves. A thousand fibres connect us with our fellow men.
Herman Melville, American writer (1819–1891)

·

Our life is love, and peace, and tenderness; and bearing one with another, and forgiving one another, and not laying accusations one against another; but praying one for another, and helping one another up with a tender hand.
[Letter to Amersham Friends Meeting, 1667]
Isaac Penington, English Quaker and writer (1617–1679)

·

No man is an island, entire of itself; every man is a piece of the continent, a part of the main.
Devotions upon Emergent Occasions (1624)
John Donne, English poet and cleric (1572–1631)

·

Mankind must put an end to war or war will put an end to mankind.
[Speech to the United Nations general assembly, 1961]
John F Kennedy, 35th president of the US (1917–1963)

·

Man, unlike any other thing organic or inorganic in the universe, grows beyond his work, walks up the stairs of his concepts, emerges ahead of his accomplishments.
The Grapes of Wrath (1939)
John Steinbeck, American writer (1902–1968)

Everything mankind does, their hope, fear, rage, pleasure,
joys, business, are the hotch-potch of my little book.
Satires
Juvenal, Roman poet (47–?)

•

Man is a bird without wings and a bird is a man without sorrow.
Birds Without Wings (2004)
Louis de Bernières, British writer (1954–)

•

We hope that the world will not narrow into a neighbourhood
before it has broadened into a brotherhood.
Lyndon B Johnson, 36th president of the US (1908–1973)

•

In all my work what I try to say is that as human beings
we are more alike than we are unalike.
New York Times (1993)
Maya Angelou, American writer (1928–2014)

•

We're born alone, we live alone, we die alone. Only through our
love and friendship can we create the illusion for the moment
that we're not alone.
Orson Welles, American actor and film director (1915–1985)

Love, hope, fear, faith — these make humanity; these are its sign and note and character.
Robert Browning, English poet (1812–1889)

•

We're all of us guinea pigs in the laboratory of God. Humanity is just a work in progress.
Camino Real (1953)
Tennessee Williams, American playwright (1911–1983)

•

I agree with you that there is a natural aristocracy among men. The grounds of this are virtue and talents.
[Letter to John Adams, 1813]
Thomas Jefferson, 3rd president of the US (1743–1826)

•

The heart of man is very much like the sea, it has its storms, it has its tides and in its depths it has its pearls too.
Vincent van Gogh, Dutch painter (1853–1890)

•

Civilisations should be measured by the degree of diversity attained and the degree of unity retained.
WH Auden, English-American poet (1907–1973)

MEN

A man's mind will very generally refuse to make itself up until it be driven and compelled by emergency.
Ayala's Angel (1881)
Anthony Trollope, English writer (1815–1882)

•

While lasting joys the man attend, who has a faithful female friend.
The Female Friend
Cornelius Whur, English clergyman and poet (1782–1853)

•

I admit it is better fun to punt than to be punted, and that a desire to have all the fun is nine-tenths of the law of chivalry.
Gaudy Night (1935)
Dorothy L Sayers, English writer (1893–1957)

•

Man is not made for defeat ... A man can be destroyed but not defeated.
Ernest Hemingway, American writer (1899–1961)

•

What would men be without women? Scarce, sir, mighty scarce.
Mark Twain, American writer (1835–1910)

The beauty myth moves for men as a mirage; its power lies in its ever-receding nature. When the gap is closed, the lover embraces only his own disillusion.
The Beauty Myth (1990)
Naomi Wolf, American writer and political advisor (1962–)

•

All women become like their mothers. That is their tragedy. No man does. That's his.
The Importance of Being Earnest (1895)
Oscar Wilde, Irish dramatist and poet (1854–1900)

•

Common sense is the most widely shared commodity in the world, for every man is convinced that he is well supplied with it.
Discours de la Méthode (1637)
René Descartes, French philosopher (1596–1650)

•

There's a man all over for you, blaming on his boots the faults of his feet.
Waiting for Godot (1953)
Samuel Beckett, Irish playwright (1906–1989)

•

Why can't a woman be more like a man?
Men are so honest, so thoroughly square;
Eternally noble, historically fair.
My Fair Lady (1951)
Alan Jay Lerner, American lyricist (1918–1986)

MISTAKES AND FAILINGS

Sometimes a person has to go a very long distance out of his way to come back a short distance correctly.
The Zoo Story (1959)
Edward Albee, American playwright (1928–2016)

.

The man who makes no mistakes does not usually make anything.
[Speech at the Mansion House, 1889]
Edward John Phelps, American layer and diplomat (1822–1900)

.

Never explain — your friends do not need it and your enemies will not believe you anyway.
The Motto Book (1907)
Elbert Hubbard, American writer (1856–1915)

.

It's a delightful thing to think of perfection; but it's vastly more amusing to talk of errors and absurdities.
Camilla (1796)
Fanny Burney, English writer and diarist (1752–1840)

.

The best of us must sometimes eat our words.
Harry Potter and the Chamber of Secrets (1998)
JK Rowling, British writer (1965–)

A man of genius makes no mistakes. His errors are volitional and are the portals of discovery.
Ulysses (1922)
James Joyce, Irish writer (1882–1941)

•

Never contradict. Never explain. Never apologise.
[Letter to *The Times*, 1919]
John Arbuthnot Fisher, 1st Baron Fisher, also known as
Jacky Fisher, British admiral (1841–1920)

•

Always acknowledge a fault. This will throw those in writerity off their guard and give you an opportunity to commit more.
Mark Twain, American writer (1835–1910)

•

It is a good rule in life never to apologise. The right sort of people do not want apologies, and the wrong sort take a mean advantage of them.
The Man Upstairs (1914)
PG Wodehouse, English writer (1881–1975)

•

There's no disaster that can't become a blessing, and no blessing that can't become a disaster.
Jonathan Livingston Seagull (1970)
Richard Bach, American writer (1936–)

I brought myself down. I gave them a sword. And they stuck it in.
[Television interview, 1977]
Richard Nixon, 37th president of the US (1913–1994)

•

I have learned more from my mistakes than from my successes.
Sir Humphry Davy, English chemist (1778–1829)

•

No snowflake in an avalanche ever feels responsible.
More Unkempt Thoughts (1964)
Stanislaw Lec, Polish satirist and poet (1909–1966)

•

I would rather feel remorse than know how to define it.
The Imitation of Christ (1418–1427)
Thomas à Kempis, Dutch-German canon regular and writer
(1380–1471)

•

Even he who is wiser than the wise may err.
Fragments
Aeschylus, Greek tragedian (542–456 BC)

MONEY AND WEALTH

Wealth is like seawater; the more we have, the thirstier
we become, and the same is true of fame.
Parerga and Paralipomena (1851)
Arthur Schopenhauer, German philosopher (1788–1860)

•

A bank is a place that will lend you money if you can prove
that you don't need it.
Bob Hope, English-born American comedian and actor
(1903–2003)

•

Economy is idealism in its most practical form.
Calvin Coolidge, 30th president of the US (1872–1933)

•

The saddest thing I can imagine is to get used to luxury.
My Autobiography (1964)
Charlie Chaplin, English comic actor, director and composer
(1889–1977)

•

If all the rich people in the world divided up their money
among themselves there wouldn't be enough to go round.
House of All Nations (1938)
Christina Stead, Australian writer (1902–1983)

A propensity to hope and joy is real riches; one to fear and sorrow, real poverty.
David Hume, Scottish philosopher (1711–1776)

.

Men seem neither to understand their riches nor their strength. Of the former they believe greater things than they should; of the latter, less.
Francis Bacon, English philosopher, statesman and essayist (1561–1626)

.

Money is like muck, not good except it be spread.
Of Seditions and Troubles (1625)
Francis Bacon, English philosopher, statesman and essayist (1561–1626)

.

Prosperity doth best discover vice, but adversity doth best discover virtue.
Essays (1625)
Francis Bacon, English philosopher, statesman and essayist (1561–1626)

.

One must be poor to know the luxury of giving.
Middlemarch (1871)
George Eliot, English writer (1819–1880)

Those who have some means think that the most important thing in the world is love. The poor know that it is money.
Thoughts in a Dry Season (1978)
Gerald Brenan, British writer (1894–1987)

•

Happy the man who, far away from business, like the race of men of old, tills his ancestral fields with his own oxen, unbound by any interest to pay.
Horace, Roman poet (65–8 BC)

•

Man must choose whether to be rich in things or in the freedom to use them.
Deschooling Society (1971)
Ivan Illich, Croatian-Australian philosopher (1926–2002)

•

If you can actually count your money, then you are not really a rich man.
The Observer (1957)
J Paul Getty, American industrialist (1892–1976)

•

If more of us valued food and cheer and song above hoarded gold, it would be a merrier world.
JRR Tolkien, English writer (1892–1973)

Anyone who has ever struggled with poverty knows how extremely expensive it is to be poor.
Fifth Avenue, Uptown (1960)
James Baldwin, American writer (1924–1987)

•

They do not easily rise out of obscurity whose talents straitened circumstances obstruct at home.
Juvenal, Roman poet (47–?)

•

She was not so much a person as an implication of dreary poverty, like an open door in a mean house that lets out the smell of cooking cabbage and the screams of children.
The Return of the Soldier (1918)
Rebecca West, British writer and literary critic (1892–1983)

•

All decent people live beyond their incomes nowadays, and those who aren't respectable live beyond other peoples.
Beasts and Super-Beasts (1914)
Saki (Hector Hugh Munro), Scottish writer (1870–1916)

•

All the arguments which are brought to represent poverty as no evil, show it to be evidently a great evil. You never find people labouring to convince you that you may live very happily upon a plentiful fortune.
Samuel Johnson, English writer, critic and lexicographer (1709–1784)

Poverty is no disgrace to a man, but it is confoundedly inconvenient.
Sydney Smith, English wit, writer and cleric (1771–1845)

•

You can be young without money but you can't be old without it.
Cat on a Hot Tin Roof (1955)
Tennessee Williams, American dramatist (1911–1983)

•

We are all Adam's children but silk makes the difference.
Thomas Fuller, English churchman and historian (1608–1661)

•

For of fortune's sharp adversity,
The worst kind of misfortune is this:
A man to have been in prosperity,
And to remember it when it is passed.
Troilus and Criseyde
Geoffrey Chaucer, English poet (c. 1343–1400)

•

Poverty is an anomaly to rich people. It is very difficult to make out why people who want dinner do not ring the bell.
Literary Studies (1879)
Walter Bagehot, British journalist, businessman and essayist (1826–1877)

A very rich person should leave his kids enough to do anything but not enough to do nothing.
Fortune (2006)
Warren Buffett, American businessman (1930–)

•

Annual income twenty pounds, annual expenditure nineteen nineteen six, result happiness. Annual income twenty pounds, annual expenditure twenty pounds ought and six, result misery.
David Copperfield (1850)
Charles Dickens, English writer and social critic (1812–1870)

•

In every well-governed state, wealth is a sacred thing; in democracies it is the only sacred thing.
Penguin Island (1908)
Anatole France, French poet (1844–1924)

•

Surplus wealth is a sacred trust which its possessor is bound to administer in his lifetime for the good of the community.
The Gospel of Wealth (1889)
Andrew Carnegie, Scottish-American industrialist (1835–1919)

•

Money speaks sense in a language all nations understand.
The Rover (1677)
Aphra Behn, English playwright (1640–1689)

MORALS AND ETHICS

There are few who would not rather be taken in adultery
than in provincialism.
Antic Hay (1923)
Aldous Huxley, English writer and philosopher (1894–1963)

•

Chastity — the most unnatural of all the sexual perversions.
Eyeless in Gaza (1936)
Aldous Huxley, English writer and philosopher (1894–1963)

•

The end cannot justify the means, for the simple and obvious
reason that the means employed determine the nature of the
ends produced.
Ends and Means (1937)
Aldous Huxley, English writer and philosopher (1894–1963)

•

To err is human, to forgive divine.
An Essay on Criticism (1711)
Alexander Pope, English poet (1688–1744)

•

What literature can and should do is change the people
who teach the people who don't read the books.
Newsweek (1995)
AS Byatt, English writer (1936–)

We have in fact, two kinds of morality, side by side: one which we preach, but do not practise, and another which we practise, but seldom preach.
Bertrand Russell, British philosopher, mathematician, historian and writer (1872–1970)

•

Boredom is ... a vital problem for the moralist, since half the sins of mankind are caused by the fear of it.
The Conquest of Happiness (1930)
Bertrand Russell, British philosopher, mathematician, historian and writer (1872–1970)

•

There are two things that will be believed of any man whatsoever, and one of those is that he has taken to drink.
Penrod (1914)
Booth Tarkington, American writer and dramatist (1869–1946)

•

For to be discontented with the divine discontent, and to be ashamed with the noble shame, is the very germ and first upgrowth of all virtue.
Health and Education (1874)
Charles Kingsley, English writer and clergyman (1819–1875)

•

The best way to get the better of temptation is just to yield to it.
Mystifications (1859)
Clementia Stirling Graham, Scottish writer (1782–1877)

Television is simultaneously blamed, often by the same people,
for worsening the world and for being powerless to change it
Clive James, Australian writer (1939–)

•

I know only that what is moral is what you feel good after
and what is immoral is what you feel bad after.
Death in the Afternoon (1932)
Ernest Hemingway, American writer (1899–1961)

•

Drive out prejudices through the door, and they will return
through the window.
Frederick the Great, King of Prussia (1712–1786)

•

An Englishman thinks he is moral when he is only uncomfortable.
George Bernard Shaw, Irish playwright (1856–1950)

•

The worst sin towards our fellow creatures is not to hate them
but to be indifferent to them; that's the essence of inhumanity.
The Devils' Disciple (1897)
George Bernard Shaw, Irish playwright (1856–1950)

•

Gossip is a sort of smoke that comes from the dirty tobacco-
pipes of those who diffuse it: it proves nothing but the bad taste
of the smoker.
George Eliot, English writer (1819–1880)

Many people genuinely do not want to be saints, and it is probable that some who achieve or aspire to sainthood have never felt much temptation to be human beings.
George Orwell, English writer (1903–1950)

•

Labour to keep alive in your breast that little spark of celestial fire called conscience.
George Washington, 1st president of the US (1732–1799)

•

Those are my principles. If you don't like them I have others.
Groucho Marx, American comedian (1890–1977)

•

Moral indignation is jealousy with a halo.
The Wife of Sir Isaac Harman (1914)
HG Wells, English writer (1866–1946)

•

Virtue knows to a farthing what it has lost by not having been vice.
Horace Walpole, English art historian and writer (1717–1797)

•

People tend to forget their duties but remember their rights.
Indira Gandhi, prime minister of India (1917–1984)

I cannot and will not cut my conscience to fit this year's fashions.
Lillian Hellman, American dramatist (1905–1984)

•

We know no spectacle so ridiculous as the British public in one of its periodical fits of morality.
Thomas Babington Macaulay, 1st Baron Macaulay, British historian and politician (1800–1859)

•

Without doubt the greatest injury of all was done by basing morals on myth. For, sooner or later, myth is recognised for what it is, and disappears. Then morality loses the foundation on which it has been built.
[Romanes Lecture, 1947]
Herbert Samuel, 1st Viscount, British politician (1870–1963)

•

One becomes moral as soon as one is unhappy.
Marcel Proust, French writer (1871–1922)

•

Always do what is right. It will gratify half of mankind and astound the other.
Mark Twain, American writer (1835–1910)

By trying we can easily learn to endure adversity.
Another man's, I mean.
Following the Equator (1897)
Mark Twain, American writer (1835–1910)

•

We never knows wot's hidden in each other's hearts;
and if we had glass winders there, we'd need keep the shutters
up, some on us, I do assure you!
Martin Chuzzlewit (1844)
Charles Dickens, English writer and social critic (1812–1870)

•

No man is a hypocrite in his pleasures.
Lives of the English Poets (1779–81)
Samuel Johnson, English writer, critic and lexicographer
(1709–1784)

•

Character is much easier kept than recovered.
Thomas Paine, English-born political activist, philosopher
and revolutionary (1737–1809)

MUSIC

Give me a laundry list and I will set it to music.
[Attr.]
Rossini, Italian composer (1792–1868)

•

Children are given Mozart because of the small quantity of the notes; grown-ups avoid Mozart because of the great quality of the notes.
My Life and Music (1961)
Artur Schnabel, Austrian pianist (1882–1951)

•

I have been told that Wagner's music is better than it sounds.
[Quoted in *The Autobiography of Mark Twain*, 1924]
Bill Nye, American humourist (1850–1896)

•

The whole trouble with a folk song is that once you have played it through there is nothing much you can do except play it over again and play it rather louder.
Music Ho! (1934)
Constant Lambert, British composer (1905–1951)

•

Playing bop is like playing Scrabble with all the vowels missing.
Look (1954)
Duke Ellington, American jazz pianist, composer and bandleader (1899–1974)

Even before the music begins there is that bored look on
people's faces. A polite form of self-torture, the concert.
Tropic of Cancer (1934)
Henry Miller, American writer (1891–1980)

•

All music is folk music. I ain't never heard no horse sing a song.
Louis Armstrong, American trumpeter (1901–1971)

•

Jazz is the only music in which the same note can be played
night after night but differently each time.
Ornette Coleman, American jazz musician (1930–2015)

•

A good song reminds us what we're fighting for.
Pete Seeger, American folk singer (1919–2014)

•

Music gives a soul to the universe, wings to the mind, flight to
the imagination, a charm to sadness, gaiety and life to everything.
Plato, Greek philosopher (c. 428/427–348/347 BC)

•

I only know two tunes. One of them is *Yankee Doodle*
and the other isn't.
Ulysses S Grant, president of the US (1822–85)

Music expresses that which cannot be said and on which it is impossible to be silent.
[Essay on William Shakespeare, 1864]
Victor Hugo, French poet, writer and dramatist (1802–1885)

•

If music be the food of love, play on.
Twelfth Night (1601)
William Shakespeare, English poet and dramatist (1564–1616)

•

Melody is the essence of music. I compare a good melodist to a fine racer, and counterpoints to hack post-horses.
Wolfgang Amadeus Mozart, Austrian composer (1756–1791)

•

The notes I handle no better than many pianists. But the pauses between the notes – ah, that is where the art resides.
Chicago Daily News (1958)
Artur Schnabel, Austrian pianist (1882–1951)

NATURE AND THE WEATHER

For nature, heartless, witless nature,
Will neither care nor know
What stranger's feet may find the meadow
And trespass there and go.
Last Poems (1922)
AE Housman, English poet (1859–1936)

•

The sea is as near as we come to another world.
North Sea off Carnoustie (1977)
Anne Stevenson, Anglo-American poet (1933–)

•

If everyone were cast in the same mould, there would be no such
thing as beauty.
The Descent of Man (1871)
Charles Darwin, English naturalist (1809–1882)

•

Disinterested love for all living creatures, the most noble
attribute of man.
The Descent of Man (1871)
Charles Darwin, English naturalist (1809–1882)

•

Everything has beauty, but not everyone sees it.
Confucius, Chinese teacher (551–479 BC)

As long as one has a garden, one has a future; and as long as one has a future one is alive.
In the Garden (1925)
Frances Hodgson Burnett, British-American writer (1849–1924)

•

If you look the right way, you can see that the whole world is a garden.
The Secret Garden (1911)
Frances Hodgson Burnett, British-American writer (1849–1924)

•

The way to ensure summer in England is to have it framed and glazed in a comfortable room.
[Letter to William Cole, 1774]
Horace Walpole, English art historian and writer (1717–1797)

•

You may drive out nature with a pitchfork, yet she'll be constantly running back.
Epistles (20 BC)
Horace, Roman poet (65–8 BC)

•

To sit in the shade on a fine day, and look upon verdure, is the most perfect refreshment.
Mansfield Park (1814)
Jane Austen, English writer (1775–1817)

When we try to pick out anything by itself, we find it hitched
to everything else in the universe.
My First Summer in the Sierra (1911)
John Muir, Scottish-American naturalist and writer (1838–1914)

•

Rain is grace; rain is the sky condescending to the earth;
without rain, there would be no life.
Self-Consciousness: Memoirs (1989)
John Updike, American writer (1932–2009)

•

Make the boy interested in natural history if you can;
it is better than games.
[In his last letter to his wife, speaking about his son Peter,
who became a celebrated naturalist]
Captain Robert Falcon Scott, British explorer (1868–1912)

•

Human subtlety … will never devise an invention more
beautiful, more simple or more direct than does nature, because
in her inventions nothing is lacking, and nothing is superfluous.
Leonardo da Vinci, Italian polymath (1452–1519)

•

In nature there are neither rewards nor punishments —
only consequences.
Some Reasons Why (1881)
Robert G Ingersoll, American lawyer (1833–1899)

Summer has set in with its usual severity.
Letters of Charles Lamb (1888)
Samuel Taylor Coleridge, English poet (1772–1834)

•

April is the cruellest month, breeding
Lilacs out of the dead land, mixing
Memory and desire, stirring
Dull roots with spring rain.
The Waste Land (1922)
TS Eliot, English-American poet, critic and dramatist (1888–1965)

•

He that plants trees loves others beside himself.
Gnomologia (1732)
Thomas Fuller, English churchman and historian (1608–1661)

•

The summer night is like a perfection of thought.
Wallace Stevens, American poet (1879)

•

Peace is always beautiful.
Leaves of Grass (1855)
Walt Whitman, American poet (1819–1892)

•

The earth is what we all have in common.
The Unsettling of America (1977)
Wendell Berry, American poet and writer (1934–)

A robin red breast in a cage
Puts all heaven in a rage.
Auguries of Innocence (1803)
William Blake, English poet (1757–1827)

•

The English climate is the vilest in the whole wide world, they
proudly proclaim, and yet they spend as much time as possible
out in it, they open their windows wide to admit it at all seasons
and they consider it the source and prime cause of all their
national virtues and characteristics.
Suffolk Summer (1948)
John Tate Appleby, American soldier (1907–1974)

•

Art is not essential where nature is sufficient.
The Hero (1637)
Baltasar Gracián, Spanish prose writer (1601–1658)

•

The kiss of the sun for pardon,
The song of the birds for mirth,
One is nearer God's heart in a garden
Than anywhere else on earth.
God's Garden (1913)
Dorothy Gurney, English writer (1858–1932)

PARENTS AND CHILDREN

Having one child makes you a parent; having two you are
a referee.
The Independent (1989)
Sir David Frost, English television host (1939–2013)

•

Birds in their little nests agree
And 'tis a shameful sight
When children of one family
Fall out, and chide, and fight.
Isaac Watts, English hymn writer (1674–1748)

•

Childhood is measured out by sounds and smells and sights,
before the dark hour of reason grows.
John Betjeman, English poet (1906–1984)

•

All happy families resemble one another, but each unhappy
family is unhappy in its own way.
Anna Karenina (1877)
Leo Tolstoy, Russian writer (1828–1910)

•

Every generation revolts against its fathers and makes friends
with its grandfathers.
The Brown Decades (1931)
Lewis Mumford, American historian (1895–1990)

When adults stop being infants, children can be children.
The Mail on Sunday (2005)
Rowan Williams, Lord Williams of Oystermouth, former
Archbishop of Canterbury (1950–)

•

Children's talent to endure stems from their ignorance
of alternatives.
Maya Angelou, American writer (1928–2014)

•

Parents learn a lot from their children about coping with life.
The Comforters (1957)
Muriel Spark, Scottish writer (1918–2006)

•

I do not think you have ever realised the shock, which the
attitude you took up caused your family and the whole nation.
It seemed inconceivable to those who had made such sacrifices
during the war that you, as their king, refused a lesser sacrifice.
[In a letter to her son, the Duke of Windsor, after he abdicated
the throne to marry the divorced Wallis Simpson, 1938]
Queen Mary, Queen consort of the United Kingdom (1867–1953)

•

Far from being the basis of the good society, the family,
with its narrow privacy and tawdry secrets, is the source
of all our discontents.
[BBC Reith Lecture, 1967]
Sir Edmund Leach, British anthropologist (1910–1989)

What did my fingers do before they held him? What did my heart do, with its love? I have never seen a thing so clear. His lids are like the lilac flower And soft as a moth, his breath. I shall not let go. There is no guile or warp in him. May he keep so.
Three Women: A Poem for Three Voices (1962)
Sylvia Plath, American poet and writer (1932–1963)

•

A child becomes an adult when he realises that he has a right not only to be right but also to be wrong.
The Second Sin (1973)
Thomas Szasz, American-Hungarian psychiatrist (1920–2012)

•

Few misfortunes can befall a boy which bring worse consequences than to have a really affectionate mother.
A Writer's Notebook (1949)
W Somerset Maugham, British playwright (1874–1965)

•

There are only two things a child will share willingly — communicable diseases and his mother's age.
[Attr.]
Dr Benjamin Spock, American paediatrician (1903–1998)

•

The thing that impresses me most about America is the way parents obey their children.
Look (1957)
Edward VIII (Duke of Windsor), King of the United Kingdom (1894–1972)

POLITICS AND POWER

As I would not be a slave, so I would not be a master.
This expresses my idea of democracy. Whatever differs
from this, to the extent of the difference, is no democracy.
Collected Works, vol 2 (1953)
Abraham Lincoln, 16th president of the US (1809–1865)

•

There is no art which one government sooner learns of another
than that of draining money from the pockets of the people.
Wealth of Nations (1776)
Adam Smith, Scottish philosopher and economist (1723–1790)

•

What is essential is the formation of the political will of the
entire nation: that is the starting point for political actions.
[Speech, 1932]
Adolf Hitler, German politician, leader of the Nazi Party and
head of Nazi Germany (1889–1945)

•

Under every stone lurks a politician.
Aristophanes, Greek playwright (450–388 BC)

I — like every politician at the federal level — am almost entirely
dependent on the media to reach my constituents … I am who
the media says I am. I say what they say I say. I become who they
say I've become.
The Audacity of Hope (2006)
Barack Obama, 44th president of the US (1961–)

•

Somewhere out in this audience may even be someone
who will one day follow in my footsteps, and preside over the
White House as the president's spouse. I wish him well!
[Remarks made at Wellesley College, 1990]
Barbara Bush, first lady of the US (1925–2018)

•

No more distressing moment can ever face a British
government than that which requires it to come to a hard,
fast and specific decision.
Barbara W Tuchman, American historian (1912–1989)

•

Every dictator uses religion as a prop to keep himself in power.
[Interview on *60 Minutes*, CBS-TV, 1986]
Benazir Bhutto, prime minister of Pakistan (1953–2007)

•

Politics are too serious a matter to be left to the politicians.
Charles de Gaulle, prime minister of France (1890–1970)

Men enter local politics solely as a result of being unhappily married.
Parkinson's Law (1958)
Cyril Northcote Parkinson, British naval historian (1909–1993)

•

A politician was a person with whose politics you did not agree. When you did agree, he was a statesman.
David Lloyd George, prime minister of the UK (1863–1945)

•

In the area of politics our major policy obligation is not to mistake slogans for solutions.
Ed Murrow, American broadcaster and journalist (1908–1965)

•

History is past politics, and politics is present history.
Methods of Historical Study (1886)
Edward Augustus Freeman, English historian (1823–1892)

•

Politicians who complain about the media are like ships' captains who complain about the sea.
Enoch Powell, British politician and scholar (1912–1998)

Elections are won by men and women chiefly because most people vote against somebody rather than for somebody.
Nods and Becks (1944)
Franklin P Adams, American journalist and humourist (1881–1960)

•

Political language ... is designed to make lies sound truthful and murder respectable, and to give an appearance of solidity to pure wind.
George Orwell, English writer (1903–1950)

•

A statesman is a politician who places himself at the service of the nation. A politician is a statesman who places the nation at his service.
Georges Pompidou, president of France (1911–1974)

•

The most radical revolutionary will become a conservative the day after the revolution.
The New Yorker (1970)
Hannah Arendt, American-German philosopher (1906–1975)

•

All the president is, is a glorified public relations man who spends his time flattering, kissing and kicking people to get them to do what they are supposed to do anyway.
[Letter to his sister in *Off the Record*, 1947]
Harry Truman, 33rd president of the US (1884–1972)

That accursed power which stands on privilege
(And goes with women, and champagne and bridge)
Broke — and democracy resumed her reign:
(Which goes with bridge, and women and champagne)
On a Great Election
Hilaire Belloc, Anglo-French writer (1870–1953)

•

Do not underestimate the determination of a quiet man.
[In a speech to the Conservative Party conference, 2002]
Iain Duncan Smith, British politician (1954–)

•

Greater love hath no man than this, that he lay down his friends
for his life.
[On Harold Macmillan sacking seven members of his cabinet in
July 1962, the Night of the Long Knives]
Jeremy Thorpe, British politician (1929–2014)

•

I do not know which makes a man more conservative —
to know nothing but the present, or nothing but the past.
The End of Laissez-faire (1926)
John Maynard Keynes, British economist (1883–1946)

•

In politics, there is no use looking beyond the next fortnight.
Joseph Chamberlain, British politician (1836–1914)

A playful moderation in politics is just as absurd as a remonstrative whisper to a mob.
The Examiner (1808)
Leigh Hunt, English poet and essayist (1784–1859)

•

Power tends to corrupt and absolute power corrupts absolutely.
[In a letter to Bishop Mandell Creighton, 1887]
Lord Acton, British historian (1834–1902)

•

Britain will be honoured by historians more for the way she disposed of an empire than for the way in which she acquired it.
New York Times (1962)
Lord Harlech, British diplomat (1918–1985)

•

We have no eternal allies, and we have no perpetual enemies. Our interests are eternal and perpetual, and those interests it is our duty to follow.
[House of Commons, 1848]
Lord Palmerston, prime minister of the UK (1784–1865)

•

The bedfellows politics made are never strange. It only seems that way to those who have not watched the courtship.
Marcel Achard, French playwright (1899–1974)

In politics if you want anything said, ask a man. If you want anything done, ask a woman.
People (1975)
Margaret Thatcher, prime minister of the UK (1925–2013)

•

Socialist governments traditionally do make a financial mess. They always run out of other people's money.
[In a television interview, 1975]
Margaret Thatcher, prime minister of the UK (1925–2013)

•

England is not all the world.
Mary Queen of Scots, Queen of Scotland (1542–1587)

•

Wickedness is the root of despotism as virtue is the essence of the Republic.
[To the revolutionary Convention, 1794]
Maximilien Robespierre, French lawyer and revolutionary leader (1758–1794)

•

The struggle of man against power is the struggle of memory against forgetting.
Milan Kundera, Czech-French writer (1929–)

Since love and fear can hardly exist together, if we must choose between them, it is far safer to be feared than loved.
The Prince (1513)
Niccolò Machiavelli, Italian diplomat and political philosopher (1469–1527)

•

In every party there is one person who, by his all-too-devout enunciation of party principles, provokes the other members to defect.
Human, All Too Human (1878)
Friedrich Nietzsche, German philosopher and writer (1844–1900)

•

We give the impression of being in office but not in power.
[Speech in the House of Commons, 1993]
Norman Lamont, British politician and chancellor of the exchequer from 1990 to 1993 in the Conservative government of John Major (1942–)

•

Politics is the art of the possible.
Otto von Bismarck, German statesman (1815–1898)

•

Tories, in short, are atrophied Englishmen, lacking certain moral and intellectual reflexes. They are recognisable, homely — even, on occasions, endearing — but liable to turn nasty at short notice.
New Statesman (1958)
Paul Johnson, English journalist and historian (1928–)

The measure of a man is what he does with power.
Plato, Greek philosopher (c. 428/427–348/347 BC)

•

What I say is that "just" or "right" means nothing but what
is in the interest of the stronger party.
The Republic
Plato, Greek philosopher (c. 428/427–348/347 BC)

•

I think a prime minister has to be a butcher and know the joints.
That is perhaps where I have not been quite competent, in
knowing all the ways that you can cut up a carcass.
The Listener
RA Butler, known as **Rab** from his initials, British politician
(1902–1982)

•

In politics you must always keep running with the pack.
The moment that you falter and they sense that you are injured,
the rest will turn on you like wolves.
RA Butler, known as **Rab** from his initials, British politician
(1902–1982)

•

I never dared be radical when young for fear it would make me
conservative when old.
Robert Frost, American poet (1874–1963)

The chancellor of the exchequer is a man whose duties make him more or less of a taxing machine. He is intrusted with a certain amount of misery which it is his duty to distribute as fairly as he can.

[Speech to the House of Commons]

Robert Lowe (Viscount Sherbrooke), British political figure (1811–1892)

•

I'm not going to rearrange the furniture on the deck of the *Titanic*.

Rogers Morton, US commerce secretary under President Ford (1914–1979)

•

Surround yourself with the best people you can find, delegate writerity, and don't interfere.

Fortune

Ronald Reagan, 40th president of the US (1911–2004)

•

Politics is supposed to be the second oldest profession. I have come to realize that it bears a very close resemblance to the first.

Ronald Reagan, 40th president of the US (1911–2004)

•

I could not dig: I dared not rob:
Therefore I lied to please the mob.
Now all my lies are proved untrue
And I must face the men I slew.

A Dead Statesman (1924)

Rudyard Kipling, English journalist and writer (1865–1936)

We all know that prime ministers are wedded to the truth,
but like other married couples they sometimes live apart.
The Unbearable Bassington (1912)
Saki (Hector Hugh Munro), Scottish writer (1870–1916)

•

I will make you shorter by a head.
[A saying]
Elizabeth I, Queen of England (1533–1603)

•

The Germans, if this government is returned, are going to pay
every penny; they are going to be squeezed as a lemon is
squeezed—until the pips squeak.
[Speech about war reparations, 1918]
Sir Eric Geddes, British politician (1875–1937)

•

An ambassador is an honest man sent to lie abroad for the
good of his country.
[Written in an album, 1606]
Sir Henry Wotton, English poet and diplomat (1568–1639)

•

People are now discovering the price of insubordination
and insurrection. And boy, are we going to make it stick!
[Referring to the coal miners' strike of 1984–85]
Sir Ian MacGregor, chairman of the National Coal Board
(1912–1998)

The way in which the man of genius rules is by persuading an efficient minority to coerce an indifferent and self-indulgent majority.
Sir James Fitzjames Stephen, British lawyer, judge and writer (1829–1894)

•

The ability to foretell what is going to happen tomorrow, next week, next month, and next year. And to have the ability afterwards to explain why it didn't happen.
[Describing desirable qualifications in a politician]
Sir Winston Churchill, prime minister of the UK, historian and Nobel Prize winner (1874–1965)

•

The great nations have always acted like gangsters, and the small nations like prostitutes.
The Guardian (1963)
Stanley Kubrick, American film director (1928–1999)

•

The most potent weapon in the hands of the oppressor is the mind of the oppressed.
[Speech in Cape Town, 1971]
Steve Biko, South African anti-apartheid campaigner (1946–1977)

•

I never saw so many shocking bad hats in my life.
[On seeing the first reformed parliament]
Arthur Wellesley, 1st Duke of Wellington, prime minister of the UK (1769–1852)

Foolish fanatics ... the men who form the lunatic fringe in all reform movements.
Theodore Roosevelt: An Autobiography (1913)
Theodore Roosevelt, 26th president of the US (1858–1919)

•

When a man assumes a public trust, he should consider himself as public property.
Thomas Jefferson, 3rd president of the US (1743–1826)

•

When the people fear the government there is tyranny;
when the government fears the people there is liberty.
Thomas Jefferson, 3rd president of the US (1743–1826)

•

If they can get you asking the wrong questions, they don't have to worry about answers.
Gravity's Rainbow (1973)
Thomas Pynchon, American writer (1937–)

•

What the proprietorship of these papers is aiming at is power, and power without responsibility — the prerogative of the harlot through the ages.
[Baldwin quoting Rudyard Kipling at an election rally, in criticism of the leading press barons of that time, 1931]
Stanley Baldwin, prime minister of the UK (1867–1947)

The House of Lords, an illusion to which I have never been able to subscribe — responsibility without power, the prerogative of the eunuch throughout the ages.
Lord Malquist and Mr Moon (1966)
Tom Stoppard, Czech-born British playwright and screenwriter (1937–)

•

Hell, I never vote for anybody. I always vote against.
WC Fields, American actor, comedian and writer (1880–1946)

•

The more you read and observe about this politics thing, you got to admit that each party is worse than the other.
Will Rogers, American actor and humourist (1879–1935)

•

You cannot fight against the future. Time is on our side.
[Speech to the House of Commons, on the Reform Bill, 1866]
WE Gladstone, prime minister of the UK (1809–1898)

•

The politicians of New York ... see nothing wrong in the rule, that to the victor belong the spoils of the enemy.
[Speech to the Senate, 1832]
William Learned Marcy, American politician (1786–1857)

Dictators ride to and fro upon tigers which they dare not dismount. And the tigers are getting hungry.
[Letter, 1937]
Sir Winston Churchill, prime minister of the UK, historian and Nobel Prize winner (1874–1965)

•

I cannot forecast to you the action of Russia. It is a riddle wrapped in a mystery inside an enigma.
[Radio broadcast, 1939]
Sir Winston Churchill, prime minister of the UK, historian and Nobel Prize winner (1874–1965)

•

The world must be made safe for democracy.
Woodrow Wilson, 28th president of the US (1856–1924)

•

America is the only idealistic nation in the world.
[Speech, 1919]
Woodrow Wilson, 28th president of the US (1856–1924)

•

No nation is fit to sit in judgment upon any other nation.
[Speech, 1915]
Woodrow Wilson, 28th president of the US (1856–1924)

SCIENCE AND TECHNOLOGY

When you are courting a nice girl an hour seems like a second.
When you sit on a red-hot cinder a second seems like an hour.
That's relativity.
News Chronicle (1949)
Albert Einstein, German theoretical physicist (1879–1955)

·

Science is an edged tool, with which men play like children,
and cut their own fingers.
Arthur Eddington, English astronomer (1882–1944)

·

Man is a tool-making animal.
Benjamin Franklin, founding father of the US (1706–1790)

·

Beautiful! Beautiful! Magnificent desolation.
[Describing the first moon walk, 1969]
Buzz Aldrin, American astronaut (1930–)

·

Science doesn't always go forwards. It's a bit like doing a
Rubik's cube. You sometimes have to make more of a mess
with a Rubik's cube before you can get it to go right.
Beautiful Minds (2010)
Dame Jocelyn Bell Burnell, Northern Irish astrophysicist (1943–)

The thing with hi-tech is that you always end up using scissors.
David Hockney, English artist (1937–)

•

One machine can do the work of fifty ordinary men.
No machine can do the work of one extraordinary man.
A Thousand and One Epigrams (1911)
Elbert Hubbard, American writer (1856–1915)

•

Almost all aspects of life are engineered at the molecular level,
and without understanding molecules we can only have a very
sketchy understanding of life itself.
What Mad Pursuit: A Personal View of Scientific Discovery (1988)
Francis Crick, British molecular biologist (1916–2004)

•

The scientist has marched in and taken the place of the poet.
But one day somebody will find the solution to the problems
of the world and remember, it will be a poet, not a scientist.
Frank Lloyd Wright, American architect (1867–1959)

•

A good scientist is a person with original ideas. A good engineer
is a person who makes a design that works with as few original
ideas as possible. There are no prima donnas in engineering.
Disturbing the Universe (1979)
Freeman Dyson, American physicist (1923–)

In questions of science, the writerity of a thousand is not worth the humble reasoning of a single individual.
Galileo Galilei, Italian polymath (1564–1642)

•

Art is meant to disturb, science reassures.
Le jour et la nuit: Cahiers 1917–1952
Georges Braque, French painter (1882–1963)

•

Science is built up of facts, as a house is built of stones; but an accumulation of facts is no more a science than a heap of stones is a house.
Science and Hypothesis (1905)
Henri Poincaré, French mathematician and philosopher of science (1854–1912)

•

Science, like art, is not a copy of nature but a recreation of her.
Science and Human Values (1956)
Jacob Bronowski, Polish-born British mathematician and science historian (1908–1974)

•

The essence of science: ask an impertinent question, and you are on the way to a pertinent answer.
The Ascent of Man (1973)
Jacob Bronowski, Polish-born British mathematician and science historian (1908–1974)

In the culture I grew up in you did your work, and did not put your arm around it to stop other people from looking. You took the earliest possible opportunity to make knowledge available.
James Black, Scottish pharmacologist and Nobel Prize winner (1924–2010)

•

It is questionable if all the mechanical inventions yet made have lightened the day's toil of any human being.
John Stuart Mill, British philosopher (1806–1873)

•

Science must begin with myths, and with the criticism of myths.
Conjectures and Refutations
Sir Karl Popper, Austrian-British philosopher and professor (1902–1994)

•

A new scientific truth does not triumph by convincing its opponents and making them see the light, but rather because its opponents eventually die, and a new generation grows up that is familiar with it.
Scientific Autobiography and Other Papers (1950)
Max Planck, German theoretical physicist (1848–1947)

•

If your experiment needs statistics, you ought to have done a better experiment.
The Mathematical Approach to Biology and Medicine (1967)
Norman TJ Bailey, English physicist (1923–)

Biology is the search for the chemistry that works.
[During a lecture in Oxford, 1966]
RJP Williams, English chemist (1926–2015)

•

To every action there is always opposed an equal reaction:
or, the mutual actions of two bodies upon each other are always
equal, and directed to contrary parts.
Principia Mathematica (1687)
Sir Isaac Newton, English mathematician (1643–1727)

•

Equations are more important to me because politics is for
the present but an equation is something for eternity.
A Brief History of Time (1988)
Stephen Hawking, English theoretical physicist (1942–2018)

•

Students accept astonishing things happening in human
genetics without turning a hair but worry about GM soya beans.
Times Higher Education Supplement (1991)
Steve Jones, Welsh geneticist (1944–)

•

Progress in science depends on new techniques, new discoveries
and new ideas, probably in that order.
Nature (1980)
Sydney Brenner, Genetic biologist (1927–)

The great tragedy of science — the slaying of a beautiful
hypothesis by an ugly fact.
Collected Essays (1893–94)
TH Huxley, English biologist (1825–1895)

•

Formerly, when religion was strong and science weak, men
mistook magic for medicine; now, when science is strong
and religion weak, men mistake medicine for magic.
The Second Sin (1973)
Thomas Szasz, American-Hungarian psychiatrist (1920–2012)

•

The outcome of any serious research can only be to make
two questions grow where one question grew before.
Thorstein Veblen, American-Norwegian economist (1857–1929)

•

It is the tension between the scientist's laws and his own
attempted breaches of them that powers the engines of science
and makes it forge ahead.
Quiddities (1987)
WVO Quine, American philosopher (1908–2000)

SEEING AND APPEARANCE

All that we see or seem
Is but a dream within a dream.
A Dream within a Dream (1849)
Edgar Allen Poe, American writer and poet (1809–1849)

•

A thing of beauty is a joy for ever:
Its loveliness increases; it will never
Pass into nothingness; but still will keep
A bower quiet for us, and a sleep
Full of sweet dreams, and health, and quiet breathing.
Endymion (1818)
John Keats, English poet (1795–1821)

•

If the doors of perception were cleansed everything would
appear to man as it is, infinite.
William Blake, English poet (1757–1827)

•

A stranger has big eyes but sees nothing.
African proverb

•

Keep up appearances; there lies the test;
The world will give thee credit for the rest.
Outward be fair, however foul within;
Sin if thou wilt, but then in secret sin.
Night (1761)
Charles Churchill, English poet (1731–1764)

SPORT AND MOTIVATION

Personally I have always looked on cricket as organised loafing.
[Attr.]
William Temple, British theologian and Archbishop
of Canterbury (1881–1944)

•

Champions keep playing until they get it right.
Billie Jean King, American professional tennis player who won
39 Grand Slam singles, doubles and mixed doubles titles (1943–)

•

If you don't have confidence, you'll always find a way not to win.
Carl Lewis, American track and field athlete who won ten
Olympic medals (1961–)

•

Ninety per cent of my game is mental. It's my concentration that
has gotten me this far.
Chris Evert, American tennis player who was ranked world No 1
for seven years (1954–)

•

An athlete cannot run with money in his pockets. He must run
with hope in his heart and dreams in his head.
Emil Zátopek, Czech runner who won four Olympic gold medals
(1922–2000)

All I've done is run fast. I don't see why people should make much fuss about that.

Fanny Blankers-Koen, otherwise known as "the flying housewife", a Dutch mother of two who won four gold medals at the 1948 London Olympics (1918–2004)

•

When anyone tells me I can't do anything, I'm just not listening any more.

Florence Griffith Joyner, American Olympic track and field champion (1959–1998)

•

All pro athletes are bilingual. They speak English and profanity.
Toronto Star (1975)

Gordie Howe, Canadian ice hockey player (1928–2016)

•

Angling may be said to be so like the mathematics, that it can never be fully learnt.
The Compleat Angler (1653)

Izaak Walton, English writer (1593–1683)

•

The medals don't mean anything and the glory doesn't last. It's all about your happiness. My happiness is just loving the sport and having fun performing.

Jackie Joyner-Kersee, American Olympic medal-winning athlete (1962–)

Four years of emotion went into those six minutes out there.
James Cracknell, English Olympic rower who won gold as part
of the coxless four in 2000 and 2004 (1972–)

•

We all have dreams, but in order to make dreams come into
reality, it takes an awful lot of determination, dedication,
self-discipline, and effort.
Jesse Owens, American track and field athlete who won four
Olympic gold medals (1913–1980)

•

Olympics — a lifetime of training for just ten seconds.
Jesse Owens, American track and field athlete who won four
Olympic gold medals (1913–1980)

•

A ball player's got to be kept hungry to become a big leaguer.
That's why no boy from a rich family ever made the big leagues.
The New York Times (1961)
Joe DiMaggio, American baseball player (1914–1999)

•

Success is a choice not a chance.
Joe Simpson, English mountaineer whose near-fatal climb in the
Andes became the subject of a book and film, *Touching the Void*
(1960–)

I called off his players' names as they came marching up
the steps behind him ... All nice guys. They'll finish last.
Nice guys. Finish last.
Leo Durocher, American professional baseball player,
manager and coach (1905–1991)

•

Putting on your first tracksuit is the best thing since sliced bread.
[On what it feels like to represent Great Britain]
Linford Christie, Jamaican-British Olympic sprinter and the first
European to break the 100 metre ten-second barrier (1960–)

•

If you want to win something, run the 100 metres. If you want
to experience something, run a marathon.
Emil Zátopek, Czech runner who won four Olympic gold medals
(1922–2000)

•

Cricket — a game which the English, not being a spiritual
people, have invented in order to give themselves some
conception of eternity.
Bees in Some Bonnets (1979)
Stormont Mancroft, 2nd Baron Mancroft, British politician and
writer (1914-1987)

•

If you fail to prepare, you're prepared to fail.
Mark Spitz, American swimmer who won seven gold medals
at the 1972 Munich Olympics (1950–)

I didn't have the same fitness or ability as the other girls, so I had to beat them with my mind.
Martina Hingis, Swiss world No 1 tennis player (1980–)

•

The moment of victory is much too short to live for that and nothing else.
The Guardian (1989)
Martina Navratilova, Czech-American professional tennis player who won 18 grand slam singles titles (1956–)

•

Just remember this: no one ever won the olive wreath with an impressive training diary.
Marty Liquori, American middle-distance runner who made the Olympic team in 1968 at age 19 (1949–)

•

A trophy carries dust. Memories last forever.
Mary Lou Retton, American Olympic gymnast (1968–)

•

Persistence can change failure into extraordinary achievement.
Matt Biondi, American Olympic swimmer (1965–)

•

Pain is something you expect. You can't win an Olympic final waving at the crowd.
Sir Matthew Pinsent, British rower who became only the fifth athlete in history to win consecutive gold medals at four Olympic Games (1970–)

To be number one, you must train like you are number two.
[On why he always trained as if he had something to prove]
Maurice Greene, American sprinter once dubbed "the fastest
man on the planet" (1974–)

•

I am building a fire, and every day I train, I add more fuel.
At just the right moment, I light the match.
Mia Hamm, American professional soccer player and Olympic
competitor in 2004 (1972–)

•

Life is … like being a sprinter: long stretches of hard work
punctuated by brief moments in which we are given the
opportunity to perform at our best.
Michael Johnson, American sprinter who won four Olympic
gold medals (1967–)

•

They don't give you gold medals for beating somebody.
They give you gold medals for beating everybody.
Michael Johnson, American sprinter who won four Olympic
gold medals (1967–)

•

You have to expect things of yourself before you can do them.
Michael Jordan, American basketball player who helped to
popularise the NBA internationally (1963–)

With so many people saying it couldn't be done, all it takes is an imagination.
[On winning his eighth Olympic gold medal of the Beijing Games]
Michael Phelps, American swimmer (1985–)

•

If you even dream of beating me you'd better wake up and apologise.
Muhammad Ali, American professional boxer, activist and philanthropist whose triumphs included winning a gold medal in the 1960 Olympics (1942–2016)

•

Sport has the power to change the world, it has the power to unite people in a way that little else does.
Nelson Mandela, president of South Africa (1918–2013)

•

When I race my mind is full of doubts — who will finish second, who will finish third?
Noureddine Morceli, Algerian athlete and 1996 Olympic medal-winner (1970–)

•

I am not interested in medals or titles. I don't need them. I need the love of the public and I fight for it.
Olga Korbut, Belarusian gymnast and four-time Olympic gold medallist (1955–)

Being a decathlete is like having ten girlfriends. You have to love them all and you can't afford to lose one.
Daley Thompson, British Olympic decathlete who won gold in 1980 and 1984 (1958–)

•

You haven't won the race, if in winning the race you have lost the respect of your competitors.
Paul Elvstrøm, Danish sailor who won four Olympic gold medals (1928–2016)

•

Nobody needs to prove to anybody what they're worthy of, just the person that they look at in the mirror. That's the only person you need to answer to.
Picabo Street, American Olympic alpine skiing champion (1971–)

•

Excellence is not a skill. It is an attitude.
Ralph Marston, American football player (1907–1967)

•

The bigger they are, the further they have to fall.
Brooklyn Daily Eagle (1900)
Robert Fitzsimmons, British boxer (1863–1917)

Even if I found out my house had burnt down when I got home
I would still be smiling.
[After winning his fourth Olympic gold medal, 2004]
Sir Matthew Pinsent, British rower who became only the fifth
athlete in history to win consecutive gold medals at four
Olympic Games (1970–)

•

It's like children ... you don't have a favourite.
[On being asked to pick his favourite Olympic win]
Sir Steve Redgrave, British Olympic rower who became the only
man to win gold medals at five consecutive Olympic Games in
an endurance event (1962–)

•

Hard work has made it easy. That is my secret.
Nadia Comăneci, Romanian gymnast and winner of three
Olympic gold medals in 1976 (1961–)

•

At one point in your life you either have the thing you want or
the reasons why you don't.
Andy Roddick, American tennis player and world No 1 (1982–)

•

Full engagement is what makes the difference between being
average and being great.
Sarah Ayton, English professional sailor who won gold in the
2004 and 2008 Olympics (1980–)

The potential for greatness lives within each of us.
Wilma Rudolph, American runner who won three gold medals
at the 1960 Rome Olympics (1940–1994)

•

My mother taught me very early to believe I could achieve any
accomplishment I wanted to. The first was to walk without braces.
Wilma Rudolph, American runner who, after contracting polio
as a child, had to walk with orthopaedic support until she was 12,
and then went on to win three gold medals at the 1960 Rome
Olympics (1940–1994)

TEMPERAMENT AND CHARACTER

You know what charm is: a way of getting the answer yes without having asked any clear question.
The Fall (1956)
Albert Camus, French philosopher, writer and journalist (1913–1960)

•

An intellectual is someone whose mind watches itself.
Carnets (1935–1942)
Albert Camus, French philosopher, writer and journalist (1913–1960)

•

Too much consistency is as bad for the mind as it is for the body. Consistency is contrary to nature, contrary to life. The only completely consistent people are the dead.
Do What You Will (1929)
Aldous Huxley, English writer and philosopher (1894–1963)

•

Those who stand for nothing fall for anything.
Alex Hamilton, British journalist (1930–2016)

•

Intelligence is quickness to apprehend as distinct from ability, which is capacity to act wisely on the thing apprehended.
Dialogues (1954)
Alfred North Whitehead, English philosopher and mathematician (1861–1947)

Comrades, this man has a nice smile, but he's got iron teeth.
[On Mikhail Gorbachev during a speech to the Soviet
Communist Party central committee in Moscow, 1985]
Andrei Gromyko, Soviet politician (1909–1989)

•

We know what happens to people who stay in the middle
of the road. They get run down.
The Observer (1953)
Aneurin Bevan, Secretary of State for Health of the UK
(1897–1960)

•

He fell in love with himself at first sight and it is a passion
to which he has always remained faithful.
[A character in *The Acceptance World*, speaking about novelist
St John Clarke, who was generally conceded to be based on
John Galsworthy, 1955]
Anthony Powell, English writer (1905–2000)

•

Our actions determine our dispositions.
Nicomachean Ethics (c. 350 BC)
Aristotle, ancient Greek philosopher and scientist (384–322 BC)

•

If passion drives you, let reason hold the reins.
Benjamin Franklin, founding father of the US (1706–1790)

I shall be an autocrat, that's my trade. And the good Lord will forgive me: that's his.
Catherine the Great, Empress of Russia (1729–1796)

•

To be nobody but yourself in a world that's doing its best to make you somebody else, is to fight the hardest battle you are ever going to fight. Never stop fighting.
A Poet's Advice (1958)
EE Cummings, American poet, painter and playwright (1894–1962)

•

Some people are moulded by their admirations, others by their hostilities.
The Death of the Heart (1938)
Elizabeth Bowen, Irish writer (1899–1973)

•

Imagine for yourself a character, a model personality, whose example you determine to follow, in private as well as in public.
Epictetus, Greek philosopher (50–135)

•

"Character," says Novalis, in one of his questionable aphorisms — "character is destiny."
The Mill on the Floss (1860)
George Eliot, English writer (1819–1880)

If a man does not keep pace with his companions, perhaps it is because he hears a different drummer. Let him step to the music which he hears, however measured or far away.
Walden (1854)
Henry David Thoreau, American writer and philosopher (1817–1862)

•

What is character but the determination of incident?
What is incident but the illustration of character?
Partial Portraits (1888)
Henry James, American writer (1843–1916)

•

A man's character is his fate.
Heraclitus, Greek philosopher (c. 540–480 BC)

•

It is not the strength of the body that counts, but the strength of the spirit.
JRR Tolkien, English writer (1892–1973)

•

A professional is a man who can do his job when he doesn't feel like it. An amateur is a man who can't do his job when he does feel like it.
[Diary entry, 1945]
James Agate, English diarist and theatre critic (1877–1947)

Talent is formed in quiet retreat, character in the headlong rush of life.
Torquato Tasso (1790)
Johann Wolfgang von Goethe, German writer and statesman (1749–1832)

•

The first test of a truly great man is his humility.
Modern Painters (1856)
John Ruskin, English art critic (1819–1900)

•

The heart prefers to move against the grain of circumstance; perversity is the soul's very life.
Assorted Prose (1965)
John Updike, American writer, art and literary critic (1932–2009)

•

The first time you meet Winston you see all his faults and the rest of your life you spend in discovering his virtues.
[On Winston Churchill in a letter to Sir Edward Marsh, 1905]
Lady Lytton, British suffragette, writer and campaigner (1869–1923)

•

He is indeed a conqueror who conquers himself.
Latin proverb

•

When it is not necessary to change, it is necessary not to change.
[Attr.]
Lucius Cary, English writer and politician (1610–1643)

A "no" uttered from the deepest conviction is better than a "yes" uttered merely to please, or worse, to avoid trouble.
Mahatma Gandhi, Indian politician, social activist and writer (1869–1948)

•

I'm extraordinarily patient provided I get my own way in the end.
Margaret Thatcher, prime minister of the UK (1925–2013)

•

The ultimate measure of a man is not where he stands in moments of comfort and convenience, but where he stands at times of challenge and controversy.
Martin Luther King Jr, American minister and civil rights activist (1929–1968)

•

Not being able to govern events, I govern myself.
Essays (1580)
Michel de Montaigne, French philosopher (1533–1592)

•

I often feel, and ever more deeply I realise, that fate and character are the same conception.
Novalis, German writer, philosopher and mystic (1772–1801)

•

Our love of what is beautiful does not lead to extravagance; our love of the things of the mind does not make us soft.
[At a funeral oration in Athens]
Pericles, Greek statesman, orator (494–429 BC)

When the fight begins within himself, a man's worth something.
Bishop Blougram's Apology (1855)
Robert Browning, English poet (1812–1889)

•

You can outdistance that which is running after you, but not
what is running inside you.
Rwandan proverb

•

Ever tried. Ever failed. No matter. Try again. Fail again.
Fail better.
Worstward Ho (1983)
Samuel Beckett, Irish playwright (1906–1989)

•

Integrity without knowledge is weak and useless, and knowledge
without integrity is dangerous and dreadful.
The History of Rasselas (1759)
Samuel Johnson, English writer, critic and lexicographer (1709–1784)

•

A healthy ear can stand hearing sick words.
Senegalese proverb

•

Tact is the knack of making a point without making an enemy.
Sir Isaac Newton, English mathematician, astronomer,
theologian, writer and physicist (1643–1727)

THE FUTURE

I never think of the future. It comes soon enough.
Albert Einstein, German theoretical physicist (1879–1955)

•

Till the sun grows cold
And the stars are old
And the leaves of the Judgment Book unfold.
Bedouin Song (1853)
Bayard Taylor, American poet, translator, diplomat and literary
critic (1825–1878)

•

The visions we offer our children shape the future. It matters
what those visions are. Often they become self-fulfilling
prophecies. Dreams are maps.
Pale Blue Dot (1995)
Carl Sagan, American astronomer and educator (1934–1996)

•

We have trained them [men] to think of the future as a promised
land which favoured heroes attain — not as something which
everyone reaches at the rate of 60 minutes an hour, whatever he
does, whoever he is.
The Screwtape Letters (1942)
CS Lewis, British literary scholar and writer (1898–1963)

The best way of predicting the future is to invent it.
[Attr.]
Alan Kay, American computer scientist (1940–)

•

The future is the only kind of property that the masters willingly concede to slaves.
The Rebel (1951)
Albert Camus, French philosopher, writer and journalist (1913–1960)

•

You can never plan the future by the past.
[Letter to a Member of the National Assembly, 1791]
Edmund Burke, Irish philosopher and statesman (1729–1797)

•

Only when one has lost all curiosity about the future has one reached the age to write an autobiography.
A Little Learning (1964)
Evelyn Waugh, English writer, journalist and book reviewer (1903–1966)

•

There is always one moment in childhood when the door opens and lets the future in.
The Power and the Glory (1940)
Graham Greene, English writer (1904–1991)

Change is the law of life. And those who look only to the past
or present are certain to miss the future.
[Address in the Assembly Hall at the Paulskirche in Frankfurt,
1963]
John F Kennedy, 35th president of the US (1917–1963)

•

Isn't it nice to think that tomorrow is a new day with no mistakes
in it yet?
Anne of Green Gables (1908)
LM Montgomery, Canadian writer (1874–1942)

•

I have seen the future; and it works.
[Letter to Marie Howe, 1919]
Lincoln Steffens, American news reporter (1866–1936)

•

Yesterday is not ours to recover, but tomorrow is ours to win
or lose.
[Thanksgiving Day address to the nation, 1963]
Lyndon B Johnson, 36th president of the US (1908–1973)

•

In your time we have the opportunity to move not only toward
the rich society and the powerful society, but upward to the
Great Society.
[Commencement address at the University of Michigan, 1964]
Lyndon B Johnson, 36th president of the US (1908–1973)

The future is called "perhaps", which is the only possible thing to call the future. And the important thing is not to allow that to scare you.

Orpheus Descending (1957)

Tennessee Williams, American playwright (1911–1983)

TIME AND THE PRESENT

Leave nothing for tomorrow which can be done today.
Abraham Lincoln, 16th president of the US (1809–1865)

·

If we want things to stay as they are, things will have to change.
The Leopard (1958)
Giuseppe di Lampedusa, Italian writer (1896–1957)

·

Every instant of time is a pinprick of eternity. All things
are petty, easily changed, vanishing away.
Meditations (c. 850)
Marcus Aurelius, Roman emperor (161–180)

·

We must use time wisely and forever realise that the time
is always ripe to do right.
Nelson Mandela, president of South Africa (1918–2013)

·

Wait for that wisest of all counsellors, time.
Pericles, Greek statesman, orator (494–429 BC)

·

History repeats itself. Historians repeat each other.
Supers and Supermen (1920)
Philip Guedalla, English barrister, historian and biographer
(1889–1944)

Here is a sort of river of things passing into being, and time is a violent torrent; no sooner is a thing brought to sight than it is swept by and another takes its place, and this too will be swept away.
Meditations (c. 850)
Marcus Aurelius, Roman emperor (161–180)

•

Time changes everything, except something within us, which is always surprised by change.
Thomas Hardy, English writer and poet (1840–1928)

•

Time has no divisions to mark its passage, there is never a thunderstorm or blare of trumpets to announce the beginning of a new month or year. Even when a new century begins it is only we mortals who ring bells and fire off pistols.
The Magic Mountain (1924)
Thomas Mann, German writer and social critic (1875–1955)

•

The innocent and the beautiful
Have no enemy but time.
In Memory of Eva Gore-Booth and Con Markiewicz (1933)
WB Yeats, Irish poet (1865–1939)

•

Summer's lease hath all too short a date.
Sonnet 18 (1609)
William Shakespeare, English poet and dramatist (1564–1616)

THOUGHT AND UNDERSTANDING

Ce qui n'est pas clair n'est pas français. What is not clear
is not French.
Discours sur l'Universalité de la Langue Française (1784)
Antoine de Rivarol, French writer (1753–1801)

•

If you would understand anything, observe its beginning
and its development.
Aristotle, ancient Greek philosopher and scientist (384–322 BC)

•

It is the mark of an educated mind to be able to entertain
a thought without accepting it.
Nicomachean Ethics (c. 350 BC)
Aristotle, ancient Greek philosopher and scientist (384–322 BC)

•

Minds are like parachutes. They only function when
they are open.
[Attr.]
Sir James Dewar, Scottish physicist (1842–1923)

•

Many people would sooner die than think. In fact they do.
The ABC of Relativity (1925)
Bertrand Russell, British philosopher, mathematician, historian,
and writer (1872–1970)

Brain: An apparatus with which we think that we think.
The Cynic's World Book (1906)
Ambrose Bierce, American writer (1842–1914)

•

What is wanted is not the will to believe, but the wish to find out,
which is its exact opposite.
Free Thought and Official Propaganda (1922)
Bertrand Russell, British philosopher, mathematician, historian,
and writer (1872–1970)

•

The real question is not whether machines think, but whether
men do.
Contingencies of Reinforcement: A Theoretical Analysis (1969)
BF Skinner, American psychologist (1904–1990)

•

Think wrongly, if you please, but in all cases think for yourself.
[Interview with Amanda Craig in *The Times*, 2003]
Doris Lessing, British writer (1919–2013)

•

There is no more dangerous error than that of mistaking the
effect for the cause: I call it the real corruption of reason.
Twilight of the Idols (1889)
Friedrich Nietzsche, German philosopher and writer (1844–1900)

TRAVEL AND RELAXATION

He who is outside his door has the hardest part of his journey behind him.
Dutch proverb

•

Railway termini. They are our gates to the glorious and the unknown. Through them we pass out into adventure and sunshine, to them, alas! we return.
Howard's End (1910)
EM Forster, English writer (1879–1970)

•

A man travels the world in search of what he needs and returns home to find it.
The Brook Kerith (1916)
George Moore, Irish writer (1852–1933)

•

One's destination is never a place, but rather a new way of seeing things.
Big Sur and the Oranges of Hieronymus Bosch (1957)
Henry Miller, American writer (1891–1980)

•

I feel about airplanes the way I feel about diets. It seems to me that they are wonderful things for other people to go on.
The Snake Has All the Lines (1958)
Jean Kerr, American writer (1922–2003)

All travelling becomes dull in exact proportion to its rapidity.
Modern Painters (1843)
John Ruskin, English art critic (1819–1900)

•

Oxford is on the whole more attractive than Cambridge to the
ordinary visitor; and the traveller is therefore recommended
to visit Cambridge first, or to omit it altogether if he cannot
visit both.
Baedeker's Great Britain (1887)

•

Whenever I prepare for a journey I prepare as though for death.
Should I never return, all is in order.
[Journal entry, 1922]
Katherine Mansfield, New Zealand writer (1888–1923)

•

The real voyage of discovery consists not in seeking new lands
but seeing with new eyes.
Remembrance of Things Past (1908)
Marcel Proust, French writer (1871–1922)

•

Each person deserves a day away in which no problems are
confronted, no solutions searched for.
Wouldn't Take Nothing for My Journey Now (1993)
Maya Angelou, American writer (1928–2014)

I believe we should all behave quite differently if we lived in a warm, sunny climate all the time.
Brief Encounter (1945)
Sir Noël Coward, English playwright (1899–1973)

•

There are only two emotions in a plane: boredom and terror.
The Times (1985)
Orson Welles, American actor and film director (1915–1985)

•

For my part, I travel not to go anywhere, but to go.
I travel for travel's sake. The great affair is to move.
Travels with a Donkey (1879)
Robert Louis Stevenson, Scottish writer (1850–1894)

•

The world is a book and those who do not travel read only one page.
St Augustine, early Christian theologian and philosopher
(354–430)

•

I haven't been everywhere, but it's on my list.
Susan Sontag, American writer, film-maker, philosopher, teacher and political activist (1933–2004)

Venice is like eating an entire box of chocolate liqueurs
in one go.
Truman Capote, American writer and actor (1924–1984)

•

You know more of a road by having travelled it than by all the
conjectures and descriptions in the world.
On The Conduct of Life (1822)
William Hazlitt, English writer and critic (1778–1830)

TRUTH

Facts do not cease to exist because they are ignored.
Proper Studies (1927)
Aldous Huxley, English writer and philosopher (1894–1963)

•

A deception that elevates us is dearer than a host of low truths.
Hero (1830)
Alexander Pushkin, Russian poet and playwright (1799–1837)

•

All falsehood is a mask; and however well made the mask
may be, with a little attention we may always succeed in
distinguishing it from the true face.
The Three Musketeers (1844)
Alexandre Dumas, French writer and dramatist (1802–1870)

•

Calumnies are answered best with silence.
Volpone (1607)
Ben Jonson, English playwright, actor, poet and literary critic
(1572–1637)

•

Now, what I want is, facts ... Facts alone are wanted in life.
Hard Times (1854)
Charles Dickens, English writer and social critic (1812–1870)

He who does not bellow the truth when he knows the truth
makes himself the accomplice of liars and forgers.
Lettre du Provincial (1899)
Charles Péguy, French poet and essayist (1873–1914)

•

The truth is on the march and nothing will stop it.
["J'accuse!" open letter, 1898]
Émile Zola, French writer (1840–1902)

•

It takes two to speak the truth — one to speak and another
to hear.
A Week on the Concord and Merrimack Rivers (1849)
Henry David Thoreau, American writer and philosopher
(1817–1862)

•

Satire is a sort of glass, wherein beholders do generally discover
everybody's face but their own.
The Battle of the Books (1704)
Jonathan Swift, Irish poet and satirist (1667–1745)

•

An exaggeration is a truth that has lost its temper.
Sand and Foam (1926)
Kahlil Gibran, Lebanese-American writer, poet and visual artist
(1883–1931)

Words that are strictly true seem to be paradoxical.
Tao Te Ching
Lao Tzu, Chinese philosopher (?–533 BC)

•

'Tis strange — but true; for truth is always strange;
Stranger than fiction.
Don Juan (1824)
George Gordon, Lord Byron, English nobleman and poet
(1788–1824)

•

If you tell the truth, you don't have to remember anything.
[Notebook entry, 1894]
Mark Twain, American writer (1835–1910)

•

Truth is the most valuable thing we have. Let us economise it.
Pudd'nhead Wilson's New Calendar (1894)
Mark Twain, American writer (1835–1910)

•

A little sincerity is a dangerous thing, and a great deal of it is
absolutely fatal.
Intentions (1891)
Oscar Wilde, Irish dramatist and poet (1854–1900)

•

The truth is rarely pure, and never simple.
The Importance of Being Earnest (1895)
Oscar Wilde, Irish dramatist and poet (1854–1900)

Truths that become old become decrepit and unreliable;
sometimes they may be kept going artificially for a certain time,
but there is no life in them.
A New Model of the Universe (1934)
PD Ouspensky, Russian philosopher (1878–1947)

•

How often have I said to you that when you have eliminated
the impossible, whatever remains, however improbable, must
be the truth?
The Sign of the Four (1890)
Sir Arthur Conan Doyle, Scottish writer (1859–1930)

VIRTUE

Forgiveness is a virtue of the brave.
Indira Gandhi, prime minister of India (1917–1984)

•

More people are flattered into virtue than bullied out of vice.
The Analysis of the Hunting Field (1846)
RS Surtees, English editor and sporting writer (1805–1864)

•

Patience: A minor form of despair, disguised as a virtue.
The Cynic's Word Book (1906)
Ambrose Bierce, American writer (1842–1914)

•

Moral virtues we acquire through practice like the arts.
Nicomachean Ethics (c. 350 BC)
Aristotle, ancient Greek philosopher and scientist (384–322 BC)

•

No one gossips about other people's secret virtues.
On Education (1926)
Bertrand Russell, British philosopher, mathematician, historian, and writer (1872–1970)

For to be discontented with the divine discontent, and to be ashamed with the noble shame, is the very germ and first upgrowth of all virtue.

Health and Education (1874)

Charles Kingsley, English writer and clergyman (1819–1875)

WISDOM AND FOLLY

Justice inclines her scales so that wisdom comes at the price of suffering.
Agamemnon (c. 490 BC)
Aeschylus, Greek tragedian (c. 525–456 BC)

•

Only a fool tests the depth of the water with both feet.
African proverb

•

Smooth seas do not make skilful sailors.
African proverb

•

All human wisdom is contained in these two words —
wait and hope.
The Count of Monte Cristo (1845)
Alexandre Dumas, French writer and dramatist (1802–1870)

•

If to talk to oneself when alone is folly, it must be doubly unwise to listen to oneself in the presence of others.
The Art of Worldly Wisdom (1647)
Baltasar Gracián, Spanish writer and philosopher (1601–1658)

Fools need advice most, but wise men only are the better for it.
Poor Richard's Almanac (1732)
Benjamin Franklin, founding father of the US (1706–1790)

•

At 20 years of age, the will reigns; at 30, the wit; and at 40,
the judgment.
Poor Richard's Almanac (1732)
Benjamin Franklin, founding father of the US (1706–1790)

•

In all affairs it's a healthy thing now and then to hang a question
mark on the things you have long taken for granted.
Bertrand Russell, British philosopher, mathematician, historian,
and writer (1872–1970)

•

By the time a man realises that maybe his father was right,
he usually has a son who thinks he's wrong.
Charles Wadsworth, American classical pianist (1929–)

•

A single conversation with a wise man is better than ten years
of study.
Chinese proverb

If one learns from others but does not think, one will be bewildered. If, on the other hand, one thinks but does not learn from others, one will be in peril.
Confucius, Chinese teacher (551–479 BC)

•

Age appears to be best in four things — old wood best to burn, old wine to drink, old friends to trust, and old authors to read.
Apophthegms New and Old (1625)
Francis Bacon, English philosopher, statesman and essayist (1561–1626)

•

One would need to be already wise, in order to love wisdom.
On the Aesthetic Education of Man (1794)
Friedrich von Schiller, German writer, philosopher and physician (1759–1805)

•

The wisest mind has something yet to learn.
George Santayana, Spanish philosopher and writer (1863–1952)

•

The ultimate result of shielding men from the effects of folly, is to fill the world with fools.
State-Tamperings with Money and Banks (1858)
Herbert Spencer, English sociologist and philosopher (1820–1903)

The motto of chivalry is also the motto of wisdom; to serve all,
but love only one.
Honoré de Balzac, French writer (1799–1850)

•

Prudent, cautious self-control, is wisdom's root.
A Bard's Epitaph (1786)
Robert Burns, Scottish poet (1759–1796)

•

There are more fools than knaves in the world, else the knaves
would not have enough to live upon.
The Genuine Remains in Verse and Prose of Mr Samuel Butler (1759)
Samuel Butler, English poet and satirist (1612–1680)

•

The wise only possess ideas; the greater part of mankind are
possessed by them.
Samuel Taylor Coleridge, English poet (1772–1834)

•

A foolish fox is caught by one leg, but a wise one by all four.
Serbian proverb

•

Let men be wise by instinct if they can, but when this fails
be wise by good advice.
Antigone (c. 441 BC)
Sophocles, ancient Greek tragedian (c. 496–406 BC)

The stupid neither forgive nor forget; the naive forgive and forget; the wise forgive but do not forget.
The Second Sin (1973)
Thomas Szasz, American-Hungarian psychiatrist (1920–2012)

•

Wisdom is sold in the desolate market where none come to buy.
The Four Zoas (c. 1797)
William Blake, English poet (1757–1827)

•

The art of being wise is the art of knowing what to overlook.
The Principles of Philosophy (1890)
William James, American philosopher and psychologist
(1842–1910)

•

This fellow's wise enough to play the fool,
And to do that well craves a kind of wit.
Twelfth Night (c. 1601–1602)
William Shakespeare, English poet and dramatist (1564–1616)

•

A fool and his words are soon parted.
On Reserve (1764)
William Shenstone, English poet and landscape gardener
(1714–1763)

WIT AND INSIGHT

Mark my words, when a society has to resort to the lavatory
for its humour, the writing is on the wall.
Forty Years On (1969)
Alan Bennett, English dramatist and actor (1934–)

•

Standards are always out of date. That is what makes them
standards.
Forty Years On (1969)
Alan Bennett, English dramatist and actor (1934–)

•

Five days shalt thou labour, as the Bible says. The seventh day
is the Lord thy God's. The sixth day is for football.
Inside Mr Enderby (1973)
Anthony Burgess, English writer (1917–1993)

•

A self-made man is one who believes in luck and sends his son
to Oxford.
House of all Nations (1938)
Christina Stead, Australian writer (1902–1983)

•

I did not fully understand the dread term "terminal illness"
until I saw Heathrow for myself.
The Sunday Times (1978)
Dennis Potter, English television dramatist and writer
(1935–1994)

There's no such thing as bad publicity except your own obituary.
My Brother Brendan (1965)
Dominic Behan, Irish songwriter and playwright (1928–1989)

•

There's a hell of a distance between wise-cracking and wit.
Wit has truth in it; wise-cracking is simply callisthenics
with words.
Paris Review (1956)
Dorothy Parker, American poet and satirist (1893–1967)

•

Anyone who isn't confused doesn't really understand
the situation.
Ed Murrow, American broadcast journalist and war
correspondent (1908–1965)

•

No grand idea was ever born in a conference, but a lot of foolish
ideas have died there.
The Crack-Up (1940)
F Scott Fitzgerald, American writer (1896–1940)

•

Years ago we discovered the exact point, the dead centre of
middle age. It occurs when you are too young to take up golf
and too old to rush up to the net.
Nods and Becks (1944)
Franklin P Adams, American columnist (1881–1960)

On the Continent people have good food; in England people have good table manners.
How to be an Alien (1946)
George Mikes, Hungarian-born British humourist and writer (1912–1987)

•

Thieves respect property. They merely wish the property to become their property that they may more perfectly respect it.
The Man who was Thursday (1908)
GK Chesterton, English writer (1874–1936)

•

The optimist proclaims that we live in the best of all possible worlds; and the pessimist fears this is true.
The Silver Stallion (1926)
James Branch Cabell, American writer (1879–1958)

•

The microwave, the waste disposal, the orgasmic elasticity of the carpets, this soft resort-style civilisation irresistibly evokes the end of the world.
America (1986)
Jean Baudrillard, French sociologist (1929–2007)

•

Three o'clock is always too late or too early for anything you want to do.
Nausea (1938)
Jean-Paul Sartre, French philosopher and writer (1905–1980)

Will the people in the cheaper seats clap your hands?
All the rest of you, if you'll just rattle your jewellery.
[Royal Variety Performance, 1963]
John Lennon, English singer, songwriter and peace activist
(1940–1980)

•

No brilliance is needed in the law. Nothing but common sense,
and relatively clean fingernails.
A Voyage Round My Father (1971)
John Mortimer, English writer, barrister and dramatist
(1923–2009)

•

A soggy little island huffing and puffing to keep up with
Western Europe.
[On England in *Picked up Pieces*, 1976]
John Updike, American writer, art and literary critic (1932–2009)

•

Here lies a great and mighty king whose promise none relies on;
he never said a foolish thing nor ever did a wise one.
[Mock epitaph for King Charles II]
John Wilmot, 2nd Earl of Rochester, English poet (1647–1680)

•

Generosity is giving more than you can, and pride is taking less
than you need.
Kahlil Gibran, Lebanese-American writer, poet and visual artist
(1883–1931)

Neurosis is a secret you don't know you're keeping.
Kenneth Tynan, English theatre critic and writer (1927–1980)

•

Good breeding consists in concealing how much we think
of ourselves and how little we think of the other person.
[Notebook, 1898]
Mark Twain, American writer (1835–1910)

•

It takes your enemy and your friend, working together, to hurt
you to the heart: the one to slander you and the other to get the
news to you.
Following The Equator (1897)
Mark Twain, American writer (1835–1910)

•

An expert is one who knows more and more about less and less.
Nicholas Murray Butler, American philosopher, diplomat and
educator (1862–1947)

•

I test my bath before I sit
And I'm always moved to wonderment
That what chills the finger not a bit
Is so frigid on the fundament.
Samson Agonistes (1942)
Ogden Nash, American poet (1902–1971)

The old believe everything, the middle-aged suspect everything, the young know everything.
Oscar Wilde, Irish dramatist and poet (1854–1900)

•

You should study the Peerage, Gerald ... it is the best thing in fiction the English have ever done.
A Woman of No Importance (1893)
Oscar Wilde, Irish dramatist and poet (1854–1900)

•

To get back my youth I would do anything in the world, except take exercise, get up early, or be respectable.
The Picture of Dorian Gray (1891)
Oscar Wilde, Irish dramatist and poet (1854–1900)

•

It is better to be beautiful than to be good. But ... it is better to be good than to be ugly.
The Picture of Dorian Gray (1891)
Oscar Wilde, Irish dramatist and poet (1854–1900)

•

Like dear St Francis of Assisi I am wedded to poverty: but in my case the marriage is not a success.
Oscar Wilde, Irish dramatist and poet (1854–1900)

All my wife has ever taken from the Mediterranean — from that whole vast intuitive culture — are four bottles of Chianti to make into lamps.
Equus (1973)
Peter Shaffer, English playwright and screenwriter (1926–2016)

•

Deprivation is for me what daffodils were for Wordsworth.
The Observer (1979)
Philip Larkin, English poet, writer and librarian (1922–1985)

•

How often does a house need to be cleaned, anyway?
As a general rule, once every girlfriend.
The Bachelor Home Companion (1987)
PJ O'Rourke, American political satirist and journalist (1947–)

•

Good manners are a combination of intelligence, education, taste, and style mixed together so that you don't need any of those things.
Modern Manners (1984)
PJ O'Rourke, American political satirist and journalist (1947–)

•

Sometimes I sits and thinks, and then again I just sits.
Punch (1906)

An autobiography is an obituary in serial form with the last instalment missing.
The Naked Civil Servant (1968)
Quentin Crisp, English writer, raconteur and actor (1908–1999)

•

The louder he talked of his honour, the faster we counted our spoons.
The Conduct of Life (1860)
Ralph Waldo Emerson, American poet, essayist and philosopher (1803–1882)

•

Any man who goes to a psychiatrist should have his head examined.
Sam Goldwyn, Polish-born American film producer (1879–1974)

•

Dull. To make dictionaries is dull work.
A Dictionary of the English Language (1755)
Samuel Johnson, English writer, critic and lexicographer (1709–1784)

•

Don't be surprised if I demur, for, be advised
My passport's green.
No glass of ours was ever raised
To toast the Queen.
[An open letter objecting to his inclusion in *The Penguin Book of Contemporary British Poetry*, 1983]
Seamus Heaney, Irish poet, playwright and translator (1939–2013)

Is it progress if a cannibal uses a knife and fork?
Unkempt Thoughts (1962)
Stanislaw Lec, Polish satirist and poet (1909–1966)

•

An original idea. That can't be too hard. The library must be full of them.
The Liar (1991)
Stephen Fry, English comedian, actor, writer and activist (1957–)

•

How gratifying for once to know that those above will serve those down below.
A Little Priest from *Sweeney Todd: The Demon Barber of Fleet Street* (1979)
Stephen Sondheim, American composer and lyricist (1930–)

•

There ain't no way to find out why a snorer can't hear himself snore.
Tom Sawyer Abroad (1894)
Mark Twain, American writer (1835–1910)

•

Eternity's a terrible thought. I mean, where's it all going to end?
Rosencrantz and Guildenstern are Dead (1967)
Tom Stoppard, Czech-born British playwright and screenwriter (1937–)

Jogging is for people who aren't intelligent enough to watch television.
Mens Sana in Thingummy Doodah (1990)
Victoria Wood, English comedian, singer and actress (1953–2016)

•

At a dinner party one should eat wisely but not too well, and talk well but not too wisely.
A Writer's Notebook (1949)
W Somerset Maugham, British playwright (1874–1965)

•

Some weasel took the cork out of my lunch.
You Can't Cheat an Honest Man
WC Fields, American actor, comedian and writer (1880–1946)

•

An expert is someone who knows some of the worst mistakes that can be made in his subject and who manages to avoid them.
Der Teil und das Ganze (1969)
Werner Heisenberg, German theoretical physicist (1901–1976)

•

Variety's the very spice of life, that gives it all its flavour.
The Task (1785)
William Cowper, English poet and hymnodist (1731–1800)

A nickname is the heaviest stone that the Devil can throw at a man.

Sketches and Essays (1839)

William Hazlitt, English writer and critic (1778–1830)

·

I am a marvellous housekeeper. Every time I leave a man, I keep his house.

Zsa Zsa Gabor, Hungarian-American actress and socialite (1917–2016)

WOMEN

We are here to claim our right as women, not only to be free,
but to fight for freedom. That it is our right as well as our duty.
Votes for Women (1911)
Christabel Pankhurst, English suffragette (1880–1958)

•

She's the sort of woman who lives for others — you can always
tell the others by their hunted expression.
The Screwtape Letters (1942)
CS Lewis, British literary scholar and writer (1898–1963)

•

Nagging is the repetition of unpalatable truths.
[Speech to the Married Women's Association, 1960]
Edith Summerskill, British physician, feminist and politician
(1901–1980)

•

A woman is like a tea bag — you can't tell how strong she is until
you put her in hot water.
Eleanor Roosevelt, first lady of the US (1884–1962)

•

I'll not listen to reason ... Reason always means what someone
else has got to say.
Cranford (1851–1853)
Elizabeth Gaskell, English writer (1810–1865)

Are simple women only fit to dress, to darn, to flower or knit,
to mind the distaff, or the spit? Why are the needle and the pen
thought incompatible by men?
A Mirror for Detractors (1754)
Esther Lewis, English poet (1716–1794)

•

The great and almost only comfort about being a woman is that
one can always pretend to be more stupid than one is and no
one is surprised.
The Valleys of the Assassins (1934)
Freya Stark, English-Italian explorer and travel writer (1893–1993)

•

The happiest women, like the happiest nations, have no history.
The Mill on the Floss (1860)
George Eliot, English writer (1819–1880)

•

I didn't fight to get women out from behind the vacuum cleaner
to get them on to the board of Hoover.
The Guardian (1986)
Germaine Greer, Australian writer and intellectual (1939–)

•

That perpetual hunger to be beautiful and that thirst to be loved
which is the real curse of Eve.
The Left Bank and Other Stories (1927)
Jean Rhys, Dominican writer (1890–1979)

Men look at women. Women watch themselves being looked at.
Ways of Seeing (1972)
John Berger, English writer and art critic (1926–2017)

•

I have met with women whom I really think would like
to be married to a poem and to be given away by a novel.
[Letter to Fanny Brawne, 1819]
John Keats, English poet (1795–1821)

•

The principle which regulates the existing social relations
between the two sexes — the legal subordination of one sex
to the other — is wrong in itself, and now one of the chief
hindrances to human improvement.
The Subjection of Women (1869)
John Stuart Mill, British philosopher and political economist
(1806–1873)

•

Women have been called queens for a long time, but the
kingdom given them isn't worth ruling.
An Old-Fashioned Girl (1870)
Louisa May Alcott, American writer and poet (1832–1888)

•

One's prime is elusive. You little girls, when you grow up, must
be on the alert to recognise your prime at whatever time of your
life it may occur.
The Prime of Miss Jean Brodie (1961)
Muriel Spark, Scottish writer (1918–2006)

I married beneath me, all women do.
Nancy Astor, American-born politician and socialite (1879–1964)

•

To ask women to become unnaturally thin is to ask them to relinquish their sexuality.
The Beauty Myth (1990)
Naomi Wolf, American writer and political advisor (1962–)

•

One should never trust a woman who tells her real age.
A woman who would tell one that, would tell one anything.
A Woman of No Importance (1893)
Oscar Wilde, Irish dramatist and poet (1854–1900)

•

I myself have never been able to find out what feminism is;
I only know that people call me a feminist whenever I express sentiments that differentiate me from a doormat or a prostitute.
Mr Chesterton in Hysterics (1913)
Rebecca West, British writer and literary critic (1892–1983)

•

The female of the species is more deadly than the male.
The Female of the Species (1919)
Rudyard Kipling, English journalist and writer (1865–1936)

Women never have young minds. They are born three thousand years old.
A Taste of Honey (1959)
Shelagh Delaney, English dramatist and screenwriter (1939–2011)

·

Few tasks are more like the torture of Sisyphus than housework, with its endless repetition: the clean becomes soiled, the soiled is made clean, over and over, day after day. The housewife wears herself out marking time: she makes nothing, simply perpetuates the present.
The Second Sex (1949)
Simone de Beauvoir, French writer (1908–1986)

·

One is not born a woman: one becomes one.
The Second Sex (1949)
Simone de Beauvoir, French writer (1908–1986)

·

Men, their rights, and nothing more; women, their rights, and nothing less.
[Motto of *The Revolution*, 1868]
Susan B Anthony, American social reformer and women's rights activist (1820–1906)

·

Varium et mutabile semper femina.
Woman is ever a fickle and changeable thing.
The Aeneid (29–19 BC)
Virgil, ancient Roman poet (70–19 BC)

Women have served all these centuries as looking glasses possessing the magic and delicious power of reflecting the figure of man at twice its natural size.

A Room of One's Own (1929)

Virginia Woolf, English writer (1882–1941)

WORDS AND WRITERS

Words calculated to catch everyone may catch no one.
[Welcome address to the Democratic National Convention, 1952]
Adlai Stevenson, American politician (1900–1965)

•

Most people ignore most poetry because most poetry ignores
most people.
Poems (1964)
Adrian Mitchell, English writer (1932–2008)

•

If your mouth turns into a knife, it will cut off your lips.
African proverb

•

I think I detect sarcasm. I can't be doing with sarcasm.
You know what they say? Sarcasm is the greatest weapon
of the smallest mind.
Woman in Mind (1985)
Alan Ayckbourn, English dramatist (1939–)

•

The greatest triumphs of propaganda have been accomplished,
not by doing something, but by refraining from doing.
Great is the truth, but still greater ... is silence about truth.
Brave New World (1932)
Aldous Huxley, English writer and philosopher (1894–1963)

Several excuses are always less convincing than one.
Point Counter Point (1928)
Aldous Huxley, English writer and philosopher (1894–1963)

•

What literature can and should do is change the people
who teach the people who don't read the books.
Newsweek (1995)
AS Byatt, English writer (1936–)

•

One man is as good as another until he has written a book.
Benjamin Jowett, English educator and theologian (1817–1893)

•

The past exudes legend: one can't make pure clay of time's mud.
There is no life that can be recaptured wholly; as it was.
Which is to say that all biography is ultimately fiction.
Dubin's Lives (1979)
Bernard Malamud, American writer (1914–1986)

•

Writers don't give prescriptions. They give headaches.
Anthills of the Savannah (1987)
Chinua Achebe, Nigerian writer (1930–2013)

If you try to nail anything down in the novel, either it kills the novel, or the novel gets up and walks away with the nail.
Phoenix: The Posthumous Papers of DH Lawrence (1936)
DH Lawrence, English writer and poet (1885–1930)

•

Poets ... though liars by profession, always endeavour to give an air of truth to their fictions.
A Treatise of Human Nature (1738)
David Hume, Scottish philosopher (1711–1776)

•

The finest eloquence is that which gets things done and the worst is that which delays them.
[Opening address, Paris Peace Conference, 1919]
David Lloyd George, prime minister of the UK (1863–1945)

•

The only books that influence us are those for which we are ready and which have gone a little farther down our particular path than we have yet got ourselves.
Two Cheers for Democracy (1951)
EM Forster, English writer (1879–1970)

•

A man who publishes his letters becomes a nudist — nothing shields him from the world's gaze except his bare skin.
[Letter, 1975]
EB White, American writer (1899–1985)

Reading without reflecting is like eating without digesting.
Edmund Burke, Irish philosopher and statesman (1729–1797)

•

I know nothing in the world that has as much power as a word.
Sometimes I write one, and I look at it, until it begins to shine.
[Letter]
Emily Dickinson, American poet (1830–1886)

•

My aim is to put down on paper what I see and what I feel in the
best and simplest way.
Ernest Hemingway, American writer (1899–1961)

•

One forgets words as one forgets names. One's vocabulary needs
constant fertilising or it will die.
The Diaries of Evelyn Waugh (1962)
Evelyn Waugh, English writer, journalist and book reviewer
(1903–1966)

•

News is what a chap who doesn't care much about anything
wants to read. And it's only news until he's read it.
After that it's dead.
Scoop (1938)
Evelyn Waugh, English writer, journalist and book reviewer
(1903–1966)

You don't write because you want to say something, you write because you have something to say.
The Crack-Up (1936)
F Scott Fitzgerald, American writer (1896–1940)

•

I suppose that so long as there are people in the world, they will publish dictionaries defining what is unknown in terms of something equally unknown.
Myles Away from Dublin (1968)
Flann O'Brien, Irish writer (1911–1966)

•

The few really great — the major novelists ... are significant in terms of the human awareness they promote; awareness of the possibilities of life.
The Great Tradition (1948)
FR Leavis, British literary critic (1895–1978)

•

Read not to contradict and confute, nor to believe and take for granted, nor to find talk and discourse, but to weigh and consider.
Essays: Of Studies (1625)
Francis Bacon, English philosopher, statesman and essayist (1561–1626)

University printing presses exist, and are subsidised by the government, for the purpose of producing books which no one can read; and they are true to their high calling.
Microcosmographia Academica (1908)
Francis M Cornford, English classical scholar and translator (1874–1943)

•

Rock journalism is people who can't write interviewing people who can't talk for people who can't read.
Loose Talk (1980)
Frank Zappa, American rock musician and songwriter (1940–1993)

•

There is a great deal of difference between an eager man who wants to read a book and the tired man who wants a book to read.
GK Chesterton, English writer (1874–1936)

•

Being published by the Oxford University Press is rather like being married to a duchess: the honour is almost greater than the pleasure.
[Letter to George Lyttelton, 1956]
GM Young, English historian (1882–1959)

•

There is a splinter of ice in the heart of a writer.
A Sort of Life (1971)
Graham Greene, English writer (1904–1991)

Human speech is like a cracked kettle on which we tap crude rhythms for bears to dance to, while we long to make music that will melt the stars.
Madame Bovary (1857)
Gustave Flaubert, French writer (1821–1880)

•

To write one's memoirs is to speak ill of everyone except oneself.
The Observer (1946)
Henri Philippe Pétain, French soldier and statesman (1856–1951)

•

Poetry is capable of saving us; it is a perfectly possible means of overcoming chaos.
Science and Poetry (1926)
IA Richards, English educator, literary critic and rhetorician (1893–1979)

•

A classic is a book that has never finished saying what it has to say.
The Uses of Literature (1980)
Italo Calvino, Italian journalist and writer (1923–1985)

•

I have always been delighted at the prospect of a new day, a fresh try, one more start, with perhaps a bit of magic waiting somewhere behind the morning.
Delight (1949)
JB Priestley, English writer, social commentator and broadcaster (1894–1984)

A true poet does not bother to be poetical. Nor does a nursery gardener scent his roses.
Le Rappel à l'ordre (1926)
Jean Cocteau, French writer and dramatist (1889–1963)

·

We tell ourselves stories in order to live.
The White Album (1979)
Joan Didion, American journalist (1934–)

·

Autobiography is now as common as adultery and hardly less reprehensible.
The Sunday Times
John Grigg, British writer, historian and politician (1924–2001)

·

A translation is no translation unless it will give you the music of a poem along with the words of it.
The Aran Islands (1907)
John Millington Synge, Irish dramatist (1871–1909)

·

The writer must be universal in sympathy and an outcast by nature: only then can he see clearly.
Flaubert's Parrot (1984)
Julian Barnes, English writer (1946–)

A critic is a man who knows the way but can't drive the car.
The New York Times Magazine (1966)
Kenneth Tynan, English theatre critic and writer (1927–1980)

•

If you can't annoy somebody with what you write, I think there's little point in writing.
Radio Times (1971)
Kingsley Amis, English writer and critic (1922–1995)

•

Philosophy is a battle against the bewitchment of our intelligence by means of language.
Philosophische Untersuchungen (1953)
Ludwig Wittgenstein, Austrian-born philosopher (1889–1951)

•

The limits of my language mean the limits of my world.
Tractatus Logico-Philosophicus (1921)
Ludwig Wittgenstein, Austrian-born philosopher (1889–1951)

•

A word after a word after a word is power.
Spelling
Margaret Atwood, Canadian writer (1939–)

•

A good book is the best of friends, the same today and forever.
Proverbial Philosophy (1838)
Martin Tupper, English writer and poet (1810–1889)

There is no surer foundation for a beautiful friendship than
a mutual taste in literature.
Strychnine in the Soup (1932)
PG Wodehouse, English writer and humourist (1881–1975)

•

What the detective story is about is not murder but the
restoration of order.
The Face (1986)
PD James, English crime writer (1920–2014)

•

I believe that political correctness can be a form of linguistic
fascism, and it sends shivers down the spine of my generation
who went to war against fascism.
Paris Review (1995)
PD James, English crime writer (1920–2014)

•

Language tethers us to the world; without it we spin like atoms.
Moon Tiger (1987)
Penelope Lively, British writer (1933–)

•

A story should have a beginning, a muddle, and an end.
New Fiction (1978)
Philip Larkin, English poet, writer and librarian (1922–1985)

Next to the originator of a good sentence is the first quoter of it.
Letters and Social Aims (1876)
Ralph Waldo Emerson, American poet, essayist and philosopher
(1803–1882)

•

There is no such thing as conversation. It is an illusion.
There are intersecting monologues, that is all.
There is No Conversation (1935)
Rebecca West, British writer and literary critic (1892–1983)

•

The newspapers! Sir, they are the most villainous, licentious,
abominable, infernal — not that I ever read them. No, I make it
a rule never to look into a newspaper.
The Critic (1779)
Richard Brinsley Sheridan, Irish satirist, playwright and poet
(1751–1816)

•

I'd as soon write free verse as play tennis with the net down.
[Interview, 1956]
Robert Frost, American poet (1874–1963)

•

The web, then, or the pattern, a web at once sensuous and logical,
an elegant and pregnant texture: that is style, that is the
foundation of the art of literature.
The Art of Writing (1885)
Robert Louis Stevenson, Scottish writer (1850–1894)

Books are good enough in their own way, but they are a mighty bloodless substitute for life.

Virginibus Puerisque (1881)

Robert Louis Stevenson, Scottish writer (1850–1894)

·

Literature is a splendid mistress, but a bad wife.

Rudyard Kipling, English journalist and writer (1865–1936)

·

Poetry is the art of uniting pleasure with truth.

A Study of Milton's Paradise Lost (1780)

Samuel Johnson, English writer, critic and lexicographer (1709–1784)

·

The only end of writing is to enable the readers better to enjoy life, or better to endure it.

Miscellaneous and Fugitive Pieces (1774)

Samuel Johnson, English writer, critic and lexicographer (1709–1784)

·

When once the itch of literature comes over a man, nothing can cure it but the scratching of a pen.

Handy Andy (1842)

Samuel Lover, Irish songwriter and composer (1797–1868)

Poetry is certainly something more than good sense, but it must
be good sense at all events; just as a palace is more than a house,
but it must be a house, at least.
Table Talk (1835)
Samuel Taylor Coleridge, English poet (1772–1834)

•

I have decided to keep a full journal, in the hope that my life will
perhaps seem more interesting when it is written down.
Adrian Mole: The Wilderness Years (1993)
Sue Townsend, English writer and humourist (1946–2014)

•

A good book is the purest essence of a human soul.
[Speech in support of the London Library, 1840]
Thomas Carlyle, Scottish historian and political philosopher
(1795–1881)

•

The good of a book lies in its being read.
The Name of the Rose (1981)
Umberto Eco, Italian philosopher, writer and professor
of semiotics (1932–2016)

•

Literature is strewn with the wreckage of men who have minded
beyond reason the opinions of others.
A Room of One's Own (1929)
Virginia Woolf, English writer (1882–1941)

Books are the mirrors of the soul.
Between the Acts (1941)
Virginia Woolf, English writer (1882–1941)

•

Let us read, and let us dance; these two amusements will never do any harm to the world.
Dictionnaire philosophique (1764)
Voltaire, French writer and philosopher (1694–1778)

•

The detective novel is the art-for-art's-sake of our yawning Philistinism, the classic example of a specialised form of art removed from contact with the life it pretends to build on. Writers, like teeth, are divided into incisors and grinders.
New Statesman (1951)
Sir Victor Sawdon Pritchett, British writer and literary critic (1900–1997)

•

We make out of the quarrel with others, rhetoric, but of the quarrel with ourselves, poetry.
Anima Hominis (1917)
WB Yeats, Irish poet (1865–1939)

•

A critic is a bundle of biases held loosely together with a sense of taste.
Dinosaurs in the Morning (1962)
Whitney Balliett, American jazz critic and book reviewer (1926–2007)

I never know what I think about something until I read what
I've written on it.
William Faulkner, American writer (1897–1962)

•

Poetry is the breath and finer spirit of all knowledge;
it is the impassioned expression which is in the countenance
of all science.
Lyrical Ballads (1798)
William Wordsworth, English poet (1771–1850)

•

Poetry is the spontaneous overflow of powerful feelings:
it takes its origin from emotion recollected in tranquillity.
Lyrical Ballads (1798)
William Wordsworth, English poet (1771–1850)

WORK AND EMPLOYMENT

The test of a vocation is the love of the drudgery it involves.
Afterthoughts (1931)
Logan Pearsall Smith, essayist and critic (1865–1946)

•

I have long been of the opinion that if work were such a splendid thing the rich would have kept more of it for themselves.
The Observer (1988)
Lord Grocott, British politician (1940–)

•

By working faithfully eight hours a day, you may eventually get to be a boss and work twelve hours a day.
Robert Frost, American poet (1874–1963)

•

It's true hard work never killed anybody, but I figure why take the chance?
The Guardian (1987)
Ronald Reagan, 40th president of the US (1911–2004)

•

Work saves us from three great evils: boredom, vice and need.
Candide (1759)
Voltaire, French writer and philosopher (1694–1778)

PEOPLE INDEX

INDEX

A

Abbey, Edward 151
Achard, Marcel 249
Achebe, Chinua 324
Acton, Lord 249
Adams, Douglas 60
Adams, Franklin P 247, 307
Adams, Henry 116, 137
Adams, John 154
Adenauer, Konrad 35
Adison, Joseph 168
Adler, Alfred 22
Aeschylus 220, 301
Agate, James 182, 279
Agathon 64
Albee, Edward 218
Albert, Prince Consort 209
Alcott, Louisa May 319
Aldrich, Henry 42
Aldrin, Buzz 259
Alexander the Great 32, 105, 193
Alfonso 148
Alfred, Lord Tennyson 159
Ali, Muhammad 128, 272
Allen, Woody 104, 188
Amis, Kingsley 42, 331
Amis, Martin 83
Angelou, Maya 53, 69, 96, 214, 242, 292
Anouilh, Jean 99, 205
Anthony, Susan B 207, 321
Apocrypha, Ecclesiasticus 135
Apollinaire, Guillaume 167
Appleby, John Tate 240
Appleton, Edward 94
Aquinas, Saint Thomas 63, 207
Arbuthnot, John 154
Archimedes 11
Arendt, Hannah 34, 247
Aristophanes 244

Aristotle 136, 277, 289, 299
Armstrong, Louis 234
Armstrong, Neil 185
Asch, Sholem 178
Ashe, Arthur 88
Astor, Mary 21
Astor, Nancy 43, 320
Atkinson, Brooks 79
Atkinson, Surgeon-Captain EL 166
Attlee, Clement 150
Atwood, Margaret 120, 331
Auden, WH 215
Augustine, St 293
Aurelius, Marcus 69, 287, 288
Austen, Jane 26, 196, 237
Auster, Paul 180
Ayckbourn, Alan 323
Ayton, Sarah 274

B

Bacall, Lauren 126
Bach, Richard 54, 185, 219
Bacon, Francis 32, 60, 137, 203, 210, 222, 303, 327
Baden-Powell, Robert 54
Bagehot, Walter 161, 191, 201, 225
Bailey, Norman TJ 262
Baldwin, James 224
Baldwin, Stanley 6, 181, 256
Balliett, Whitney 336
Balzac, Honoré de 112, 304
Banksy 93
Bareham, Lindsey 47
Barker, Ronnie 141
Barnes, Julian 196, 330
Barr, Amelia Edith 202
Barrie, JM 74, 89
Baudrillard, Jean 308
Bauer, Yehuda 163